SKYWAY

By
Jim Curtis

Photography: Gene Page, Phil Skinner, Sandy Gray & T.P. O'Neill

Jim Curtis, 1802 Bedford Terrace H176, Sun City Center, FL 33573.

Skywayjim1980@gmail.com

ISBN: 978-169568121-7

Chillum Publishing, Ltd.

To the victims of the Skyway Bridge disaster, may they rest in peace.

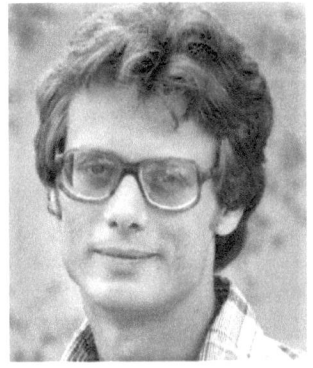

Jim Curtis was bureau chief of the Sarasota Herald-Tribune's Bradenton newsroom in 1980. Curtis learned of the Skyway Bridge collision minutes after it occurred and, thinking the call a prank, went back to bed. A second call minutes later confirmed the unbelievable had happened. Curtis, with news team in tow, rushed to the top of the Skyway and watched the rescue operation. He coordinated the news bureau's coverage in the following days and weeks.

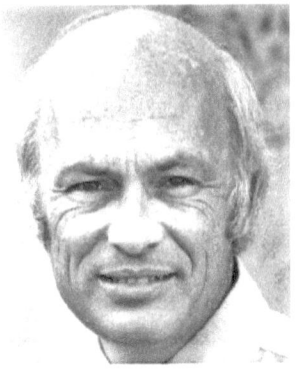

Gene Page was a veteran photojournalist and a Sarasota Herald-Tribune staff photographer. A half-hour after the Skyway fell, Page was aboard a speedboat that outraced the Coast Guard to the scene. Page managed to shoot dozens of exclusive photographs before the Coast Guard cleared the scene.

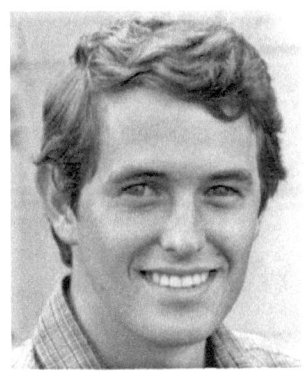

Phil Skinner began his professional career at 19. Skinner, a Sarasota Herald-Tribune photographer, stationed himself on the northbound span the morning of May 9, 1980 and captured on film the day's events from beginning to end.

Table of Contents

Chapter 1
Skyway Bound

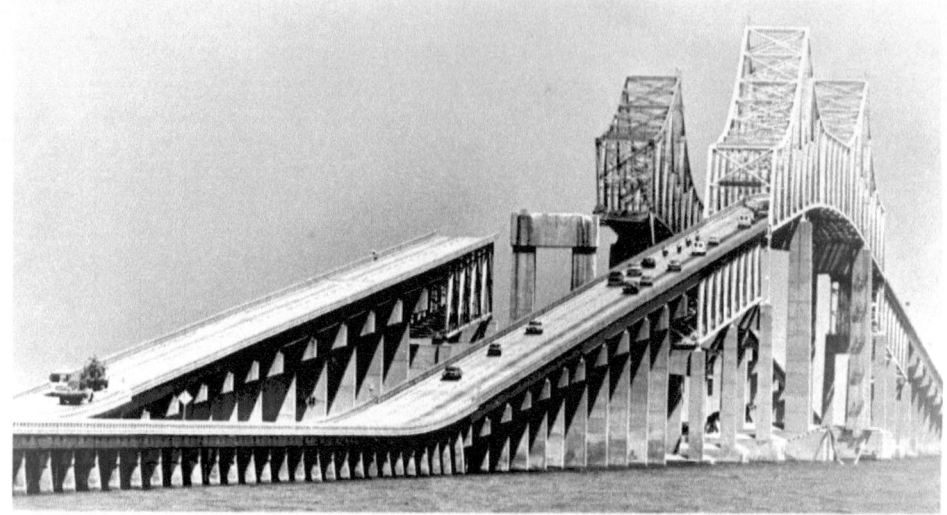

Eleven miles east of Egmont Key the Skyway spreads its massive concrete piers. Coming in from the Gulf, the pilots take aim, shoot for the gap, put their vessels on the other side and make the slow easy turn north to the ports of Tampa.

Friday, May 9, 5:43 a.m.

The anchors of the *Summit Venture* break the surface of the Gulf of Mexico and the giant ship steams slowly toward Egmont Key, the kidney-shaped Island at the mouth of Tampa Bay, Florida. She Is behind schedule. The local harbor pilot was to board at 5 a.m. but Capt. Hsuing Chu Lui said no. Visibility was so poor he could not see the bow of this ship.

But now, finally, in a business where time Is money, the *Summit Venture* is under way, ready to begin the last leg of her long voyage. She sailed from Japan with a cargo of steel and off-loaded at Houston. She left the Texas Gulf coast on Monday, May 5, and made the crossing in two days, dropping anchor at the approach of the Tampa Bay shipping channel late Tuesday afternoon. She remained there at anchor for almost three days, waiting for an open berth at the busy Port of Tampa. While waiting, the captain ordered her water ballast pumped out. Now, as she moves toward the sheltered bay, her belly is empty. She rides light, her bow stuck in the air at a snooty angle, ready to take on 28,000 tons of Florida phosphate. Then she will sail out of port and begin the long return journey to Asia.

A 55-foot boat races out to meet the *Summit Venture*. On board are John Lerro and Bruce Atkins, the pilot and co-pilot assigned to guide the freighter up the channel and into port. At 4 a.m. they received their wake-up calls at their cottages on Egmont Key and reported to duty at the pilot's station.

As Lerro walked through the darkness the wind blew a heavy mist against his finely chiseled face. Once inside the station he scanned the long line of blackboards against the wall and checked his assignment. Limping noticeably, he moved his compact frame to the reference library and read from Lloyd's Registry. The *Summit Venture*, 608 feet long, 19,734 tons, 50 feet high; the pilothouse is 510 feet from the bow, leaving 98 feet to the stern. Owned by Hercules Carriers, Ltd., it is registered In Monrovia, Liberia.

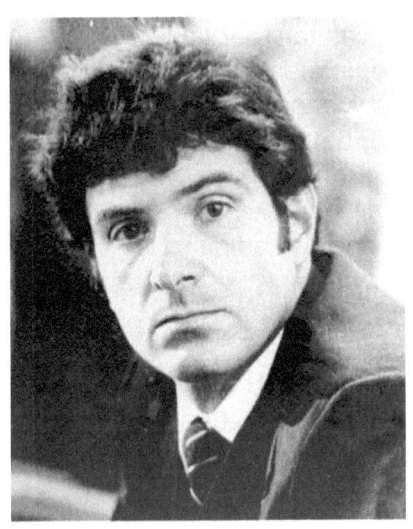

John Lerro

A Tampa Bay pilot can expect to make $75,000 per year, an indication he is one of the chosen, one of the 18 pilots and four deputies who possess the right amount of sea savvy.

A standard freighter. Lerro has piloted hundreds just like it in his ten years on the Panama Canal and in his three years on Tampa Bay.

Lerro listened to the radio scanner and gleaned information from other pilots about the weather and the conditions on the bay. The rain, wind and limited visibility come from a storm in the Gulf of Mexico. It has been building all night. At 4:22 a.m. it was 100 miles offshore and moving up the coast in a northeasterly direction.

6:25 a.m.

The bow of the *Summit Venture* cuts through aquamarine Tampa Bay. The pilot boat circles and with a burst of speed catches up with the big ship. The pilot maneuvers the customized craft into place and matches the speed of the *Summit Venture*.

He gently nestles the pilot boat against the hull of the massive freighter and with skillful piloting makes it stick there like a leech.

Lerro and Atkins make ready to board the *Summit Venture*. They move toward the edge of a platform high atop the pilot boat. First one then the other reaches out and grasps the rope ladder to climb up the side of the ship. The wind is blowing, it is misting, and there is a chop on the bay – hazardous conditions for making a circus-like boarding onto a vessel the length of two football fields. One behind the other they ascend the ladder hand over hand. The freighter is riding light and it is a long haul up the face of the ship, but the boarding comes off without a hitch.

Capt. Lui, the ship's master, relinquishes control to Lerro, the pilot, who bestows his authority on Atkins, the pilot trainee. A 1970 graduate of the U.S. Maritime Academy and a 10-year veteran captain on Gulf Oil Company tankers, Atkins is on board to complete the last of his 30 days as a trainee for the Tampa Bay Pilots' Association, a group of seafarers who monopolize the guiding of vessels in and out of port.

Upon completion of this four-hour, 42-mile journey, Atkins becomes eligible for membership as a deputy pilot and the advantages it brings. There is the opportunity to put roots In the Tampa Bay community, an upbeat metropolis where the living is easy.

The working conditions are tolerable – 21 days on, 21 off. And then there is the money. A Tampa Bay pilot can expect $75,000 per year, an indication he is one of the chosen, one of those 18 pilots and four deputies who possesses the right amount of sea savvy.

And a pilot needs sea savvy to take a giant hunk of floating metal up and down a bay that is nothing more than an estuary with a ditch down its gut. Slip out of the channel and – wap, hard aground, a monumental embarrassment to most pilots but a common occupational hazard to the pilots who navigate Tampa Bay. To complicate matters, to prove a pilot Is blessed with the most salty of sea savviness, an obstacle is in the way

3

– the Sunshine Skyway, 10 miles of bridge and causeway spanning the bay and connecting St. Petersburg with cities to the south. Eleven miles east of Egmont Key, the Skyway spreads its massive concrete piers. Coming in from the Gulf, the pilots take aim, shoot for the gap, put their vessels on the other side and make the slow easy turn north to the ports of Tampa.

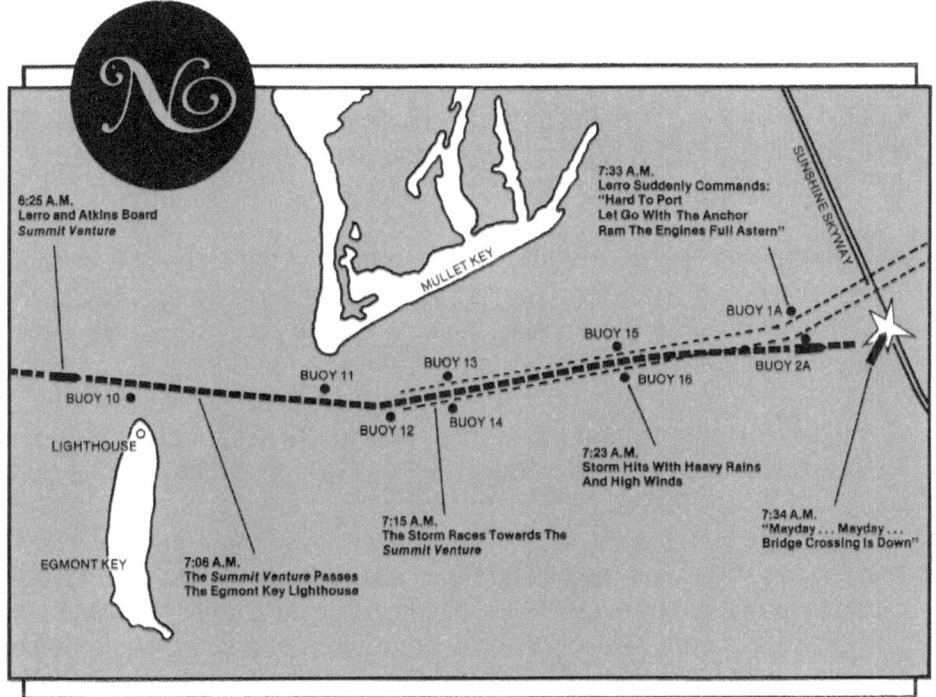

SKYWAY BOUND

To pass this test – the association believes in making its pilots learn by doing – Atkins, under the supervision of Lerro, must bring the *Summit Venture* through a series of buoys until he reaches a point seven-tenths of a mile west of the Skyway. Here he must make a sharp northeasterly turn to slip the ship beneath the straddling columns of the twin-spanned Skyway.

From the pilothouse Atkins spots the light tower on the northern tip of Egmont. It is 7:06 a.m. Atkins looks ahead for the quick flashing light at buoy 11. It flashes so rapidly it is on more than off. It signals the pilots to beware.

Quick flashing 11 marks the approach to the Mullet Key channel. Steer straight at the buoy and risk being met head-on by an outgoing vessel. The trick is to find the buoy to the south, number 12, with its 2½-second red flash that marks the channel for incoming vessels. The radar screen, set on a three-mile scan, shows an outbound ship approaching, the Good Sailor out of Port Manatee.

As the *Summit Venture* nears buoy 12, Atkins orders the helmsman to steer a few degrees north, swinging the bow of the ship left, placing it squarely in the channel. The *Summit Venture* radios the pilot of the 350-foot Good Sailor to make sure all is well. The ships pass uneventfully. By now, the mist turns to rain, reducing visibility to three or four miles. The sun, inhibited by the nasty weather, is a faint glow in the east.

Now Atkins and Lerro have time to prepare for the Sunshine Skyway. There is no hurry. The critical turn is almost three miles away. The *Summit Venture* is steaming full ahead, and it will be a full 15 minutes before Atkins must take aim for the bull's-eye between the bridge.

Coming up quickly on port side is the flashing green light of buoy 13 and to starboard unlit 14. Then comes the long straight cruise to 15 and 16 and preparations to shoot the gap.

The chart reveals 16 is the critical buoy. Its red beacon flashes every four seconds. Its bell rings. Pay attention. High above in the pilothouse of the *Summit Venture* the bell is inaudible. No matter. In a straight line behind 16 is the range – a series of lights that direct pilots toward the crucial 2A, the buoy marking that all-important turn to port less than a mile from the Skyway.

Trying to draw a bead on 2A without the range lights is like trying to draw a perfectly horizontal line through one point. Success depends on the point of reference.

Begin too many degrees to the north and the line slopes downhill as it moves east. Start too far south and it goes uphill. Without being able to verify the simple geometry provided by the range light on the bridge and two others to the east, pilots lose that indispensable peace of mind of knowing they are following a course that will thread their ships through the hole in the bridge.

7:15 a.m.

In less than three hours the storm has traveled 100 miles. Now it moves into Tampa Bay, covering it with dark dense clouds. First mist, then drizzle, and now a rain so hard driving that John Lerro takes command from his trainee. The ship cruises past buoy 14 to port and the intensity of the rain drives Lerro to action. He has been a professional pilot for 14 of his 37 years and he knows the impact of rough weather. He orders the engines cut to half speed ahead.

In the dining room of the *Summit Venture* Sit Hau Po, 60, a seafarer for 38 years, breakfasts. The call from the pilothouse comes that the boatswain mate is needed. Po leaves his meal to stand dead center on the bow. In minutes Po spots the flashing red light of 15 and radios the sighting to the pilothouse via intercom.

Lerro steps from the pilothouse and sees 16 pass starboard. He looks ahead for the flashing of 2A and the distant range lights, but the rain drops a curtain of water. He sends a message for the lookouts to watch for the starboard buoy, 2A, the most crucial of the turn buoys.

To successfully slip the *Summit Venture* through the hole, Lerro must wait until the bow nears the vertical plane of the two buoys. He must order the helmsman to come to the next course, 063, seventeen degrees to the north. The course must be maintained until the *Summit Venture* penetrates and ruptures the 800-foot hole in the bridge, sending the ship safely to the spaciousness beyond. A mistake means the ship will move too far left or too far right. Lerro will be faced with the horrendous burden of avoiding the gigantic concrete pillars that keep the Skyway's roadbed 150 feet above the bay. But, as incredible as it may seem, Lerro has faced this burden before.

<center>~~~</center>

Lerro will be faced with the horrendous burden of avoiding the gigantic concrete pillars that keep the Skyway's roadbed 150 feet above the bay. But, as incredible as it may seem, Lerro has faced this burden before.

<center>~~~</center>

It is February 16, 1980, a Saturday, and the bridge is loaded with cars bearing out-of-state plates – Michigan, Ohio, New York – snowbirds who flock to Florida to flee the frozen North. Lerro is piloting the Jonna Dan, a

6

720-foot freighter headed to the Port of Tampa to take on a load of citrus pellets. The eastbound channel is blocked by a salvage vessel anchored 30 feet above the U.S. Coast Guard cutter Blackthorn, lying on the bottom since the night of January 28, when it collided with an oil tanker just west of the Skyway. The Blackthorn took 23 of its 50 crewmen down with it. Many of the bodies remain trapped in the vessel as it lies on its port side, not far from turn buoy 2A.

The shipping channel had been closed while marine authorities wrestled with the problem of raising the Blackthorn and its dead. The bustling ports all along the bay were idled. The moans of shipping interests grew louder daily as they tabulated losses in the millions. A compromise was reached. Establish a temporary channel. Let vessels alternate. Inbound, outbound. The pilots, those men with sea savvy, they can navigate through the makeshift mousehole beneath the bridge.

It's clear, it's calm, and Lerro takes the Jonna Dan north of the temporary buoy marking the temporary channel. The Jonna Dan gives the salvage vessel and the wreck wide berth, staying far to the left. Too far.

The freighter is slow in negotiating a turn back to the right. The margin of error has been exceeded. Not only will the ship miss the bull's-eye, but there is the terrifying possibility it will miss the whole target. The monstrous hulk of floating metal is aimed at the support columns of the Skyway. Lerro's sea savvy is within minutes of desalinization.

Drop the anchors, he orders. The freighter's momentum yanks out yards of chain. Smoke pours off the anchor brakes. The bow stops short of the hole. But then the wind and current go to work, pushing the stern clockwise. A cluster of wooden pilings bound by rusty cables stands in the way. The Jonna Dan mows them down like toothpicks tied with thread. Its port side slams the pier. Tons of lateral pressure push against the legs of a bridge engineered for vertical strength.

Lerro calls for help. A nearby tug answers. As it works to dislodge the freighter, motorists stop on the high-speed roadway. They lean over the Skyway's railings, craning their necks for a better view of a potential disaster in the making. Their own.

The tug swings the stern about. With both anchors dragging, the Jonna Dan eases under the Skyway and through the hole. It leaves behind a

$40,000 mistake – a gash two inches deep, four inches wide and 10 feet long. No injuries, except to John Lerro's pride.

~~~

7:25 a.m.

Capt. Lui is in the pilothouse of the *Summit Venture*, studying the radar screen. It is cluttered with atmospheric interference, but he makes out a train of yellow lights – the Sunshine Skyway Bridge.

Sit Hau Po, joined by two other lookouts, remains in position on the bow. Visibility is so poor he cannot yet spot the turn buoys.

Meanwhile, west of Egmont Key, the Good Sailor moves into the open Gulf. Pilot Earl Evans stands on the bridge with his captain and watches the storm race toward them. It grows by the minute and Evans puts the Good Sailor on dead slow. The rage of the storm engulfs them, and the air explodes with intense thunder and lightning. The fury of the storm knocks the captain into Evans. The wind whips the water with gale force, but the Good Sailor takes it head-on. Visibility is nil. The storm is moving up the channel now, closing in on the *Summit Venture*.

Atkins peers into the *Summit Venture's* radar screen and waits for the turn buoys to appear. The screen is fuzzed out and all he can do is wait and hope. Then, momentarily, the screen clears. "We have them," Atkins calls out. "We're in the channel where we're supposed to be." Then the radar screen goes blank.

On the eastside of the dual-spanned bridge John Schiffmacher pilots the *Pure Oil* westward toward the hole in the bridge. Radio contact with the *Summit Venture* has been established and the pilots are aware of one another. The *Pure Oil* headed to Texas with its belly full is within three miles of the hole.

The storm makes it appear as though the sun failed to rise this morning. From the pilothouse the bow has disappeared, swallowed by the black curtain of rain.

Atkins fiddles with the radar but the screen remains blank. Where are the turn buoys? Lerro must know. And he must know now. His mind races ahead, quickly studying the options.

He can instruct the helmsman to steer a hard-left rudder, swing the bow counterclockwise, and wait it out at anchor. But that might put the *Summit Venture* in the outbound channel, and the *Pure Oil* is up ahead.

A starboard turn? Swing clockwise. Drop anchor or run aground? The *Summit Venture* is riding high, pulling only 21-feet of water. The captain dumped the ballast while at anchor. It is too far to the shallows. The bridge is close. With 29 feet of freeboard showing, the wind will blow the ship like a balloon. With no one holding the string.

"Where are the turn buoys?"

The answer arrives instantaneously. *"Buoy starboard bow. Buoy starboard bow."* *"Where on the starboard bow?"*

Lerro shoots back. *"I have to know where."* Capt. Lui radios the bow. It dawns on Lerro the ship has to be within 50 feet of the buoy for the lookout to see it through the blackness.

"Come to the next course," he commands.

Atkins instructs the helmsman to steer 063 degrees north. The Chinese helmsman repeats the order in English and Atkins hears the steering instrument click into place.

Seven-tenths of a mile to the hole in the bridge. The tension eases in the pilothouse.

Wind-whipped rain lashes Sit Hau Po on the bow. He holds his position and stares into the gloom. Suddenly he sees a faint outline, nothing more than shadowy lines. He squints harder. It is the bridge. Looming dead ahead. He calls his discovery to the pilothouse.

Lerro feels the *Summit Venture* skirting across the bay like a crab. The force of the wind is grabbing the ship and pushing it laterally. Lerro tells the captain to order Po and the lookouts to stand by the anchor. There is an urgency in the pilot's voice, a tone that gives Lui a sense of foreboding.

Lerro orders the speed cut to slow ahead. The hole has to be there any minute. Lerro moves the binoculars from his face, ready to issue orders should a last-second correction in course be necessary.

He stares ahead into the curtain of rain, waiting for the hole in the bridge to show itself. Then, suddenly, from the corner of his eye – light, from a rip in the curtain, illuminating the shadowy lines of steel girders: The Sunshine Skyway Bridge!

Lerro grabs the telegraph and signals the engine room. Then coolly, calmly, with the right amount of sea savvy: "**HARD TO PORT... LET GO WITH THE ANCHOR...RAM THE ENGINES FULL ASTERN.**"

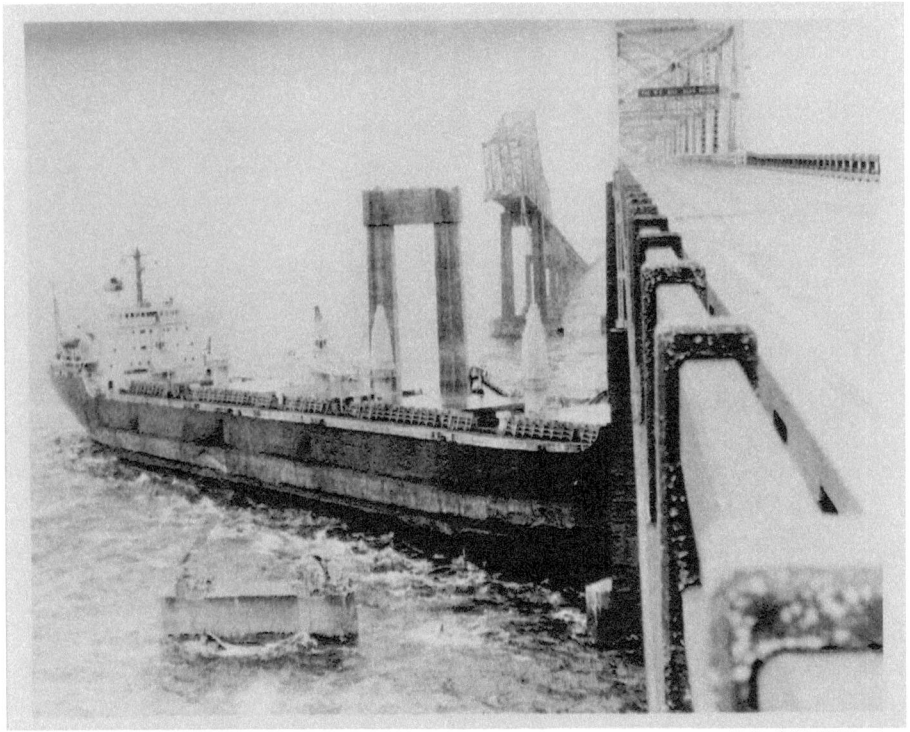

T.P. O'Neill Photo

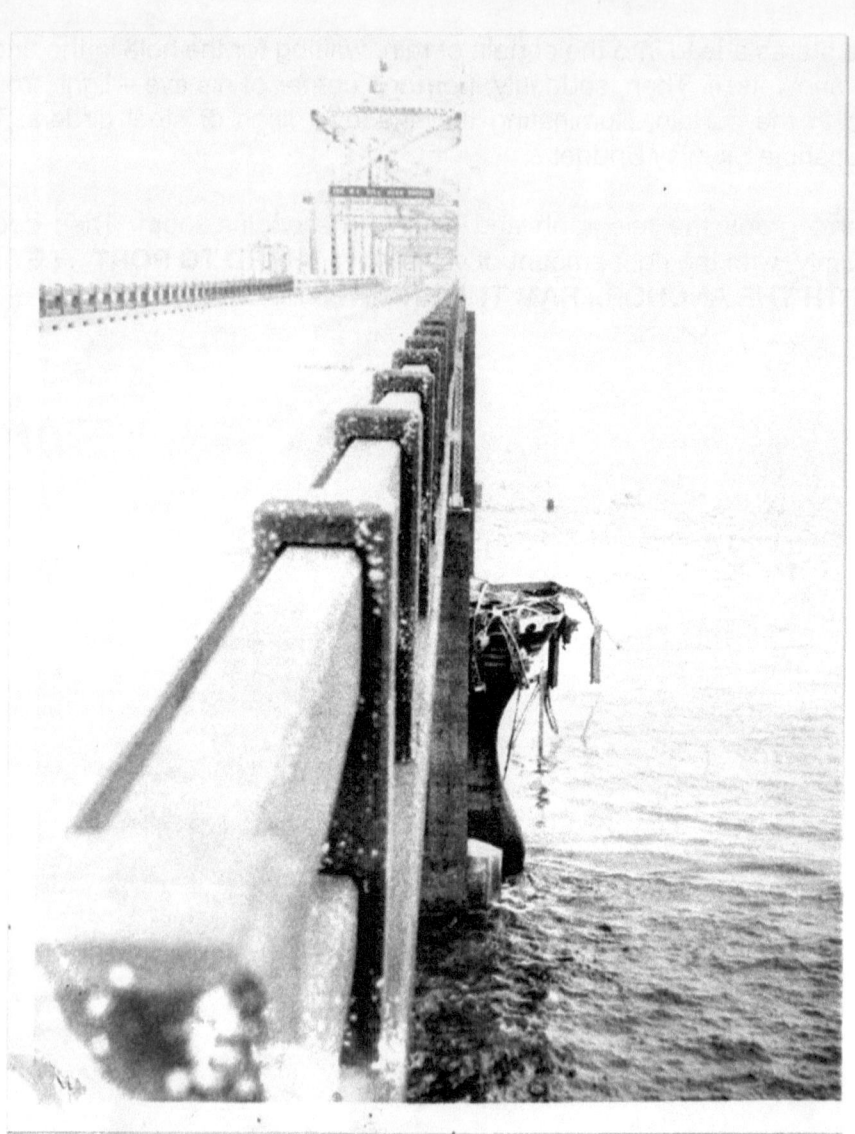

T.P. O'Neill Photo

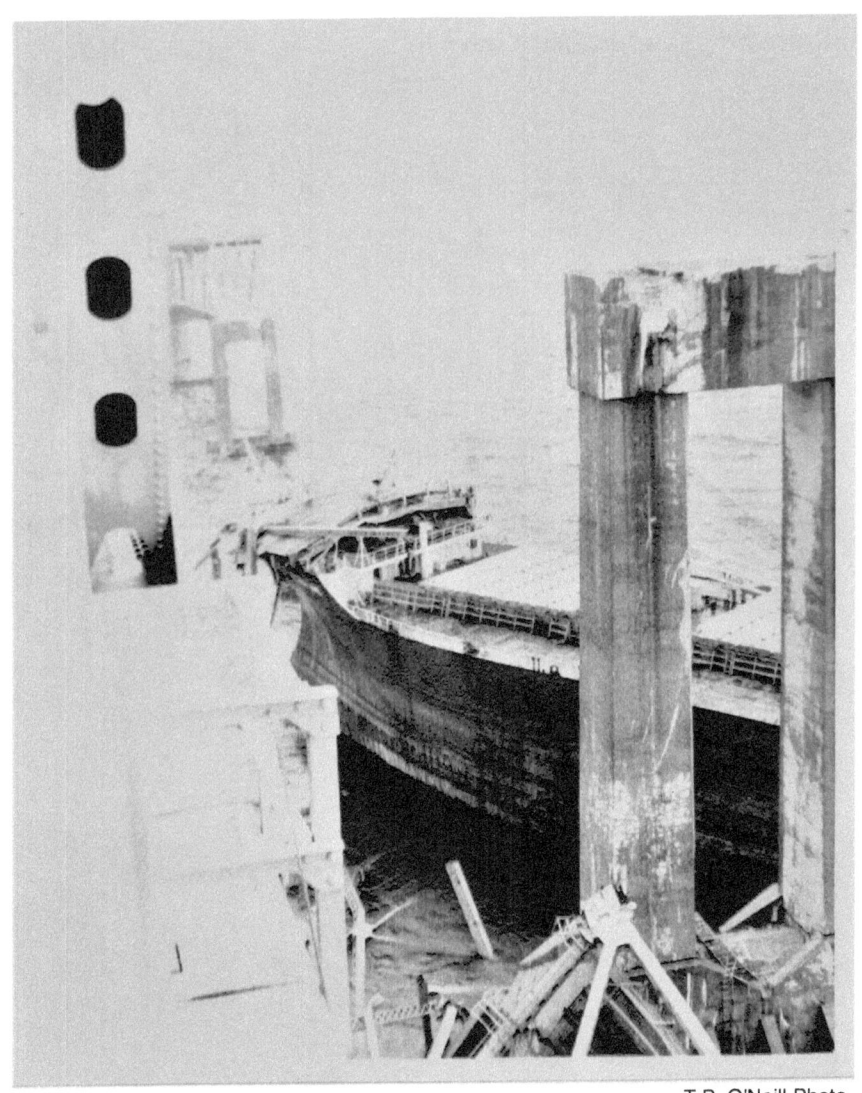

T.P. O'Neill Photo

The storm is gone, the sky is clear, and, in the distance, John Schiffmacher witnesses the incredible: A quarter mile of the southbound span has disappeared.

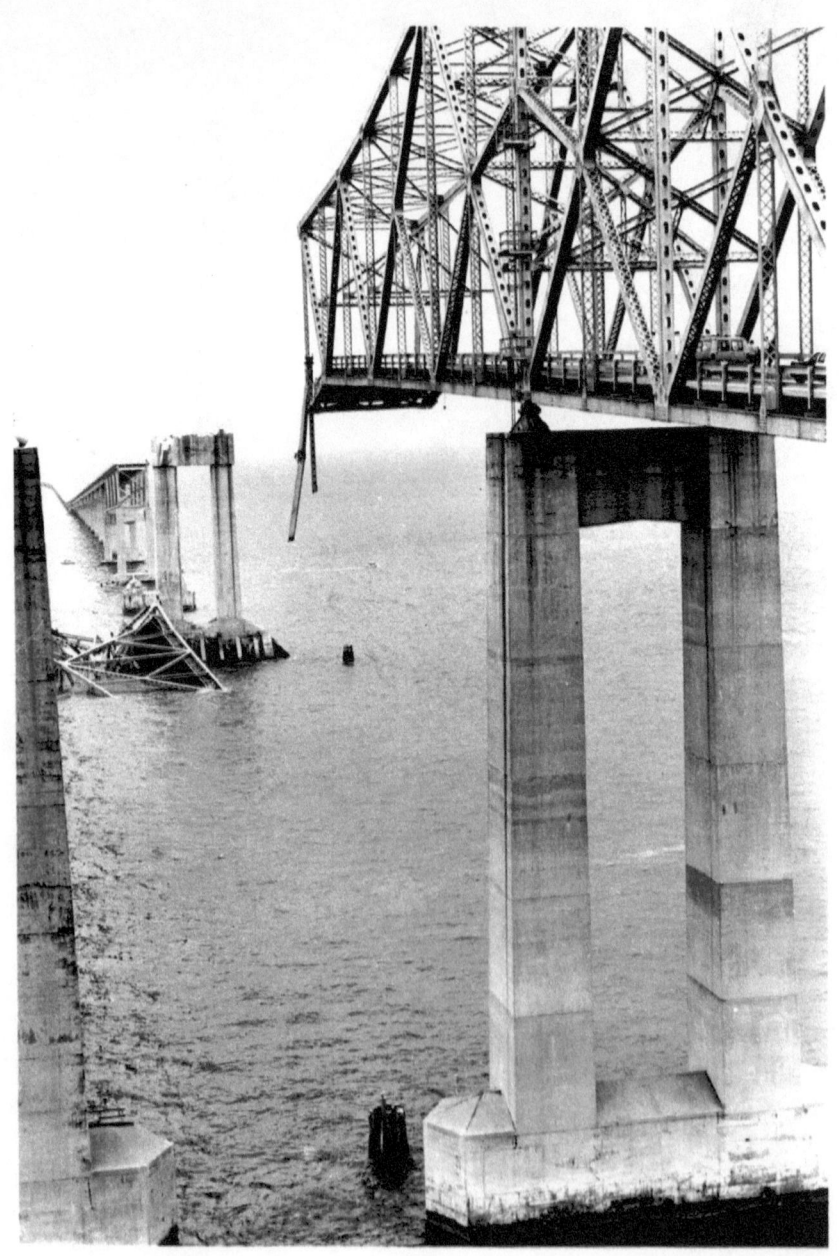

13

Chapter 2
The Victims

Margurite Mathison steps into the Friday morning drizzle. Clutching a small suitcase and an overnight bag, she waves goodbye to her friend in the car and reminds him of her return next week. She turns and heads for the bus that will carry her from St. Petersburg to Miami and the cruise ship docks there.

It has been a rough week for Margurite. It is not easy being the widowed owner of an apartment complex, especially at her age, 82, and in her condition. Two hip operations limit her mobility and she spend most of her time in her tiny apartment in downtown St. Petersburg. She has spent too much time in the dark rooms crammed with memories, and now she looks to escape. When life gets her down, she has the means and the gumption to pick up and fly away. She flies spiritually, never physically. For Margurite is scared to death of airplanes. Despite the discomfort in her hips, she feels sprightly enough to endure the seven-hour bus ride to Miami. Then she will board a ship and relax on the cruise to Nassau.

§ § § §

Friday morning marks the end of a week's vacation on St. Petersburg Beach for the Browns and the Hudsons, two Canadian couples from Newfoundland.

Thursday night they telephoned the taxi company to make sure a driver will arrive on time to take them to the St. Petersburg bus depot. Shortly after 6 a.m. the taxi pulls up. Willis and Myrtle Brown bunch into the taxi with Aubrey and Phyllis Hudson for the ride downtown and the waiting bus – the 7:05 a.m. Greyhound bus to Miami. Through the pre-dawn morning the city of St. Petersburg looks gray and miserable. It is a good day to end a stay at the beach.

§ § § §

Wanda McGarrah is excited. She is halfway in her bus trip from Tallahassee to Miami. She will be spending Sunday, Mother's Day, with her mother in Ft. Lauderdale. Then she can start preparing for Wednesday's surprise birthday party for her mother. And her mother, like all grandmothers, will be delighted to see little Monisha, six months.

Monisha. Such a beautiful name. Wanda and Charles thought about that name for five years. And now as Wanda moves through the St. Petersburg bus station, she carries a beautiful bundle befitting of its name. Wanda's bright mood is tinged with a blueness when she thinks of her husband Charles. She wanted him to come along, but he had to stay in Tallahassee. She will call Charles when she and Monisha arrive in Ft. Lauderdale. Surely, he will be able to come for Wednesday's surprise party.

§ § § §

Like Wanda McGarrah, Tawanna McClendon boarded the bus in Tallahassee. A 20-year-old student at Tallahassee Community College, Tawanna is headed home to Palmetto for Mother's Day. It is going to be a joyous celebration, for Tawanna has made it through another school year. As the Greyhound roars down the coast toward Tampa Bay, Tawanna is drawn closer to the reunion she knows is waiting. Her family will hug her, kiss her, show her through an outpouring of affection the pride her strength and courage brings them.

Though her tall, graceful exterior radiates an ebony beauty, inside it is being ravished by sickle cell anemia. In the last couple of years Tawanna spent more time in a hospital room than a classroom. But she carries on, rarely complaining, preferring to stifle her pain and continue her studies. She possesses an internal fortitude, a strong silent will that refuses to let the debilitating disease win out.

And now, with another school year almost behind her, she is heading home to her family, her fiancé, triumphant that she is successful where others fail.

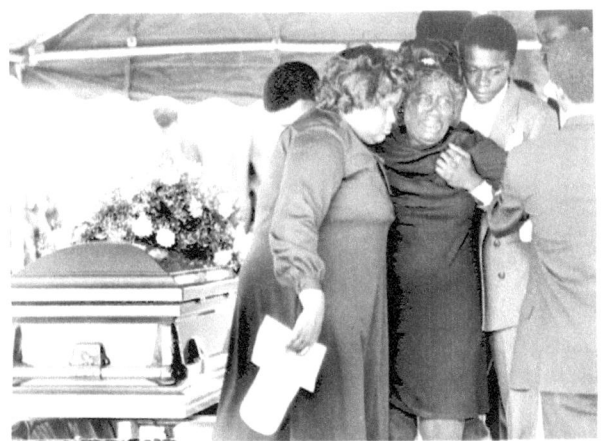

Phil Skinner Photo

16

Duane Adderly, 21, telephones the Miami home of Linda Daniels, his 20-year-old girlfriend. He tells the Daniels family he and Linda are catching the first bus, that they will be home later that afternoon.

They could have been there already if they could have afforded airplane tickets. But money comes hard to college students and on Thursday, Duane and Linda boarded the bus in Montgomery, Alabama. The ride has been more bearable because three of their Tuskegee Institute classmates are headed home, too. John Callaway, a 20-year-old engineering student, is on the bus. So are Sharon Dixon and Yvonne Johnson. School is finished but Sharon and Yvonne still wear their Tuskegee T-shirts, a sign of the contagious school spirit they all share. There they are, together, as the bus rolled south from hilly Montgomery, through the Panhandle to Tallahassee, and on into the night until it finally reaches St. Petersburg.

§ § § §

Passengers come; passengers go. So do drivers as the Greyhound continues toward the last leg of its 1,200-mile trek. The bus leaves Chicago 11:30 Wednesday night and makes major stops in Louisville, Nashville, Birmingham, and Montgomery. The passengers change, the drivers change, but through those 31 grueling hours Mel Russell stays with the bus. And now, as the bus prepares to leave the St. Petersburg depot, he is 90 minutes from his wife Julie and their seven-year-old.

It has been a month since the separation. Mel, 37, an out-of-work truck driver, stayed in Chicago. Julie and the boy went to Sarasota where Julie's sister lives. Sarasota is the shimmering Jewel of the West Coast. If Mel likes it, the family will start anew there.

§ § § §

Mike Curtin leaves his Apollo Beach home on the eastside of the Tampa Bay and makes the familiar drive to the St. Petersburg bus station. Curtin, 43, an 11-year veteran of Greyhound, is to take the next leg of the journey – St. Petersburg to Miami and back again.

As he waits for the passengers to board, he chats with a colleague, the driver who sits behind the wheel of the express to Miami. A woman approaches. She is confused. Both buses go to the same place. One takes the coastal route, the other the inland highway. Which shall she take?

Curtin and his buddy exchange good natured barbs. Curtin can offer the woman the glorious vistas of Tampa Bay and the tropical scenery of the towns and cities that dot the Gulf Coast. She even will get to see the Everglades. From the window of the express bus she will see only cows and palmetto bushes. Curtin loses the argument when the woman learns she can save an hour on the express.

Curtin knows the express is quicker and he turns professional when two young women board prior to departure. They are Canadian college students touring the country. Nice girls headed to Ft. Lauderdale. Take the express, Curtin tells them, you'll save an hour.

Minutes later Curtin eases the big bus and its 22 passengers onto the city streets. Next stop, Bradenton, the first sizeable city south of Tampa Bay.

§ § § §

By 7:20 a.m. U.S. 19 is beginning to swell with traffic. The bridge runners, those motorists who use the Sunshine Skyway to commute to and from work, are out in force. Down the ribbon of highway they come, stopping at the tollbooths on the northside of the Skyway. One-by-one they pay their 50 cents, wait for the green light to flash, and then they are off – 10 miles of uninterrupted driving over one of the most gorgeous stretches of highway in the world.

But today they will be without the Skyway's awe-inspiring panorama. The bay is locked-in by fog. Rain limits visibility further. On days like this it is best to concentrate on your driving and the taillights ahead.

§ § § §

Wesley MacIntire's blue mini-pickup truck is in the parade of cars that streams forth from the tollgates. MacIntire is an experienced bridge runner. Every weekday he crosses twice: in the morning to his mechanic's job near Bradenton and then home to Gulfport. Some people cringe when they ascend the steep incline of the Skyway and hear the tires whine on the metal grating of the superstructure 15 stories above the bay. But to MacIntire and the other bridge runners the Skyway is a part of daily living.

§ § § §

Richard Hornbuckle has crossed the Skyway more times than he can count. He is not a regular, though. This morning's crossing is special. Hornbuckle and his three passengers are headed for Avon Park to pick up cars for a St. Petersburg auto dealer. Today Hornbuckle must cross the bridge and make the long drive to Central Florida. Tomorrow morning about this time he will be engaging in the only driving he really enjoys – off the tees of a golf course. An avid golfer, Hornbuckle carries his clubs in the trunk of his yellow Buick Skylark.

§ § § §

Jim Pryor became a bridge runner when he accepted a better job in Bradenton. That was seven years ago. He decided to keep his family in their suburban St. Petersburg home. His son graduates from high school next month and maybe things will change. For now, Pryor makes the long drive in his El Camino truck. Right now, though, he is late. For some reason he forgot to put out the trash for the garbage men. In the rush-rush of the morning's routine he lost a few precious minutes when he had to turn around and drive back home to complete his chore.

§ § § §

Harry and Hildred Dietch cross the Skyway regularly. The elderly couple goes to Bradenton about every ten days. Hildred's favorite hairdresser is there. She will not let anyone else touch her hair. This trip is special. Hildred wants to look especially nice because company is arriving. Their daughter and son-in-law are flying in from Louisiana for Mother's Day. Harry will run Hildred to Bradenton in their Ford LTD and she'll return looking lovely.

§ § § §

Terry Butterfield reaches the tollbooth at 7:30 a.m. The weather is horrid. The wind whips the rain sideways. Butterfield piddled around this morning and he will have to race the clock to reach his high school teaching post on time. If the rain slackens, he can make better time. But from the look of things, it is doubtful. Never has he seen such vicious weather in his daily travels over the Skyway. Butterfield pushes on, keeping pace with traffic, 30 to 35-mlles-per-hour in a 55-miles-per-hour zone.

§ § § §

Betty McCoy rolls into the tollbooth a few minutes before 7:30 a.m. She knows she is late, and she knows she must make good time from here to Bradenton or else someone will have to babysit her students at the elementary school. She gains a minute or two just before the bridge. Ordinarily, she stops at O'Neill's Skyway Boat Basin to pick up another teacher. But not today.

19

In her 11 years of bridge running she has seen nasty weather. Sometimes the wind blows so hard she feels the superstructure sway. The wind is not so bad this morning, she thinks, but it is eerie out there – dark, foggy and drizzling. She passes O'Neill's on the right and drives onto the two-lane bridge. Traffic slows considerably and she pulls into the passing lane. Her car noses up the sharp incline that leads to the peak, and soon her tires hum to the vibrations from the metal grating of the roadway. A long line of vehicles stretches out behind her, including Wesley MacIntire's pickup truck; Jim Pryor's El Camino; the yellow Ford LTD carrying Harry and Hildred Dietch; Don Albritton's light blue Chevy Nova; Richard Hornbuckle's yellow Buick Skylark; the Greyhound bus with its 23 occupants; and, bringing up the rear, the young high school teacher, Terry Butterfield.

As McCoy nears the end of the superstructure, she feels a tremor. It is a queer feeling, totally different from the sensation of the bridge bending in the breeze. No longer are there headlights behind her.

§ § § §

Sit Hua Po receives the order from the pilot house to let go with the anchor. He triggers the mechanism and the ship spits out anchor chain. Instantly the fog is parted by a massive concrete pillar looming high above the ship's bow. Po braces himself and waits for the inevitable. The *Summit Venture* slips silently ahead. Suddenly the air explodes with shattered concrete and steel.

Lerro feels a halt to the ship's forward motion. Vibrations run the length of the vessel and jar the men in the pilothouse. They are knocked off-balance, but they remain upright. Lerro glances up. His worst nightmare Is being played before his eyes. The steel superstructure twists away and falls from its supports like a severed clothesline. Hundreds of yards of roadway and steel girders plummet into the green-gray bay. Through the black fury of the storm Lerro sees twin orbs of light dropping into the water. He grabs the radio and calls for help. It is 7:34 a.m. Friday, May 9, 1980, the day the Skyway fell.

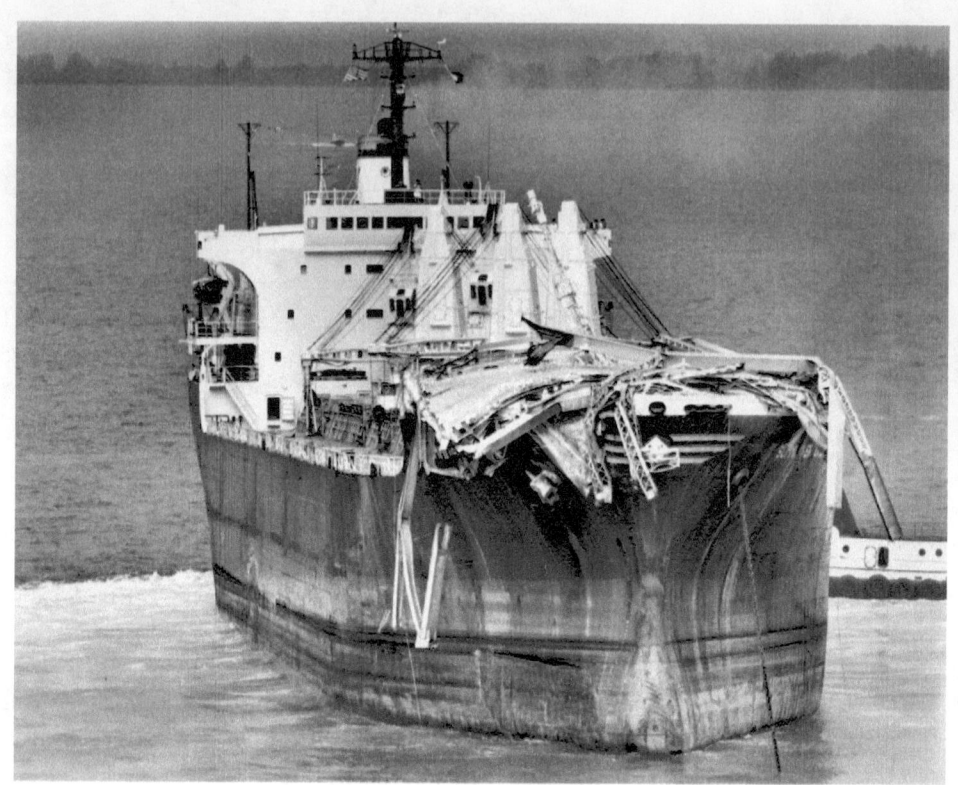

Sandy Gray Photo

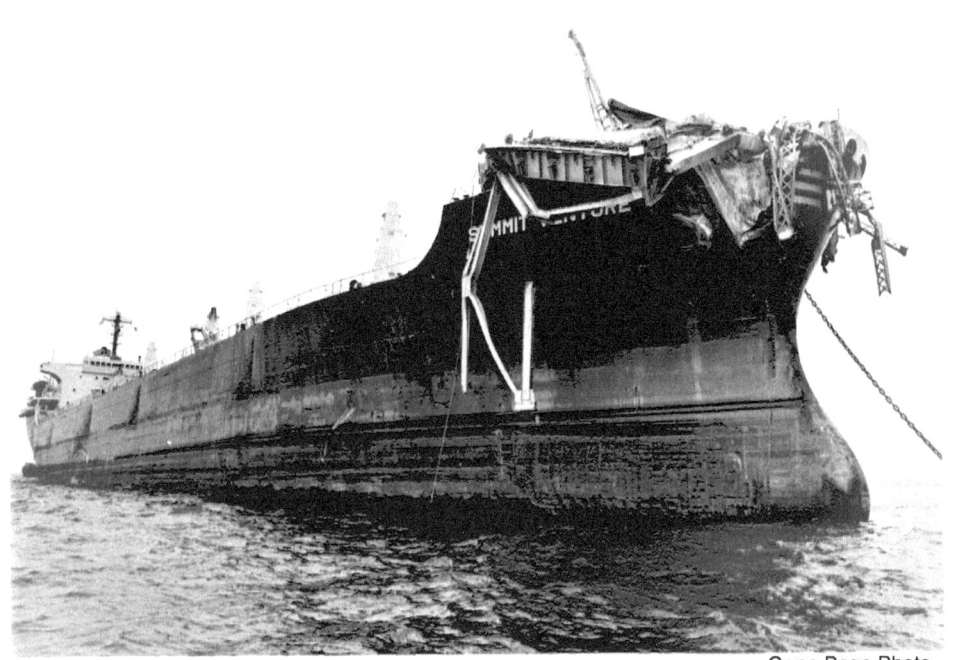

The rain falls so furiously that Wesley MacIntire's windshield wipers cannot keep pace. He considers stopping on the Skyway. He is near the peak and decides to proceed. As he reaches the zenith, the center line slithers like a snake. The roadway Is crumbling ahead of him. MacIntire stomps on the brake pedal; the wheels lock, the tires begin to slide. The truck pitches forward and noses downward with the roadway. A length of roadway five cars long falls across the *Summit Venture's* bow. The pickup comes down with it, bounces, and falls back into the water.

Far behind MacIntire, the wheels of Don Albritton's Chevy Nova reach the metal grating of the superstructure. Far ahead, Albritton sees the giant girders falling from the sky. Then he feels the bridge begin to tremble and quake. He slams on his brakes, throws the car into reverse, and begins backing down the incline toward St. Petersburg. After several hundred yards he sees headlights approaching from the rear, and he stops. He lays on the horn, waves his arms, and screams as the cars drive past.

§ § § §

Hornbuckle creeps toward the top of the bridge, clenching the wheel to fight off gusts of wind and driving rain. His speed is down to 20. Two cars pull ahead in the left lane and leave the yellow Buick behind. Hornbuckle sees Albritton's car in the right lane and stops a safe distance away.

The Greyhound bus goes by in the left lane. Hornbuckle pulls out, eases around the Chevy and follows the taillights of the bus up the steep incline. The bus goes over the peak and its lights disappear. Hornbuckle reaches the peak and the tires whine on the metal grating of the roadway. Hornbuckle sees no trace of the bus's taillights up ahead. Suddenly he is peering into the gray nothingness of the horizon. Where is the bridge? There Is nothing ahead but space.

Hornbuckle feels the Buick nose downward. He jumps on the brake pedal. The Buick's tires bite into the tiny metal studs protruding from every square inch of the metal grating. Hornbuckle feels the car slide sideways down the lip of the limply hanging roadway. The Buick's front wheels stop 14 inches from the ragged edge where 1,260 feet of roadway are ripped away. Hornbuckle and his stunned passengers stare at the bay 15 stories below. All four doors fly open and the men scramble out onto the rain-slick metal grating; they fight to keep their footing as they climb up the dangling piece of bridge, struggling against the wind-whipped rain, straining to save their lives by gaining safety on the undamaged roadway 20 yards ahead.

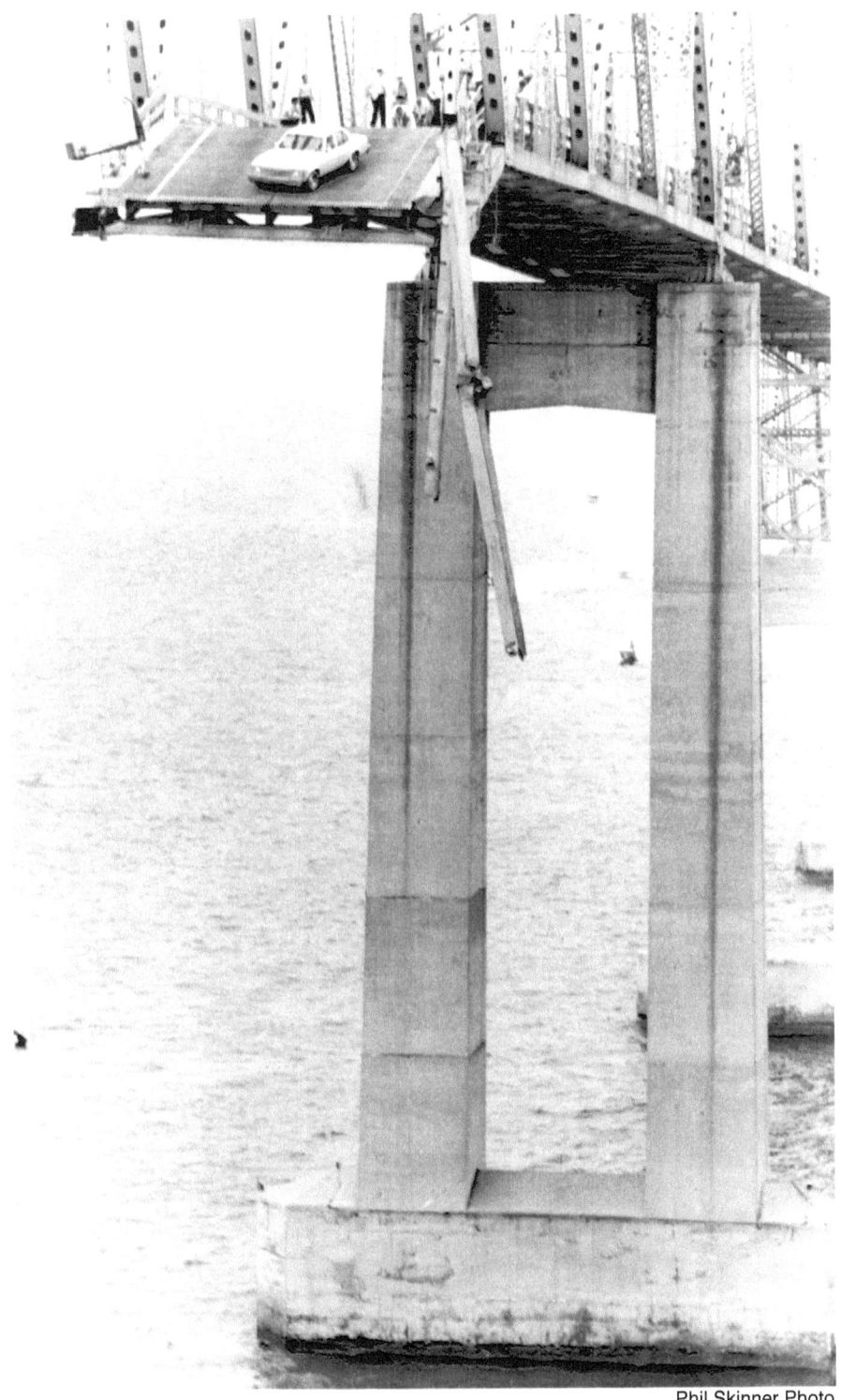

Phil Skinner Photo

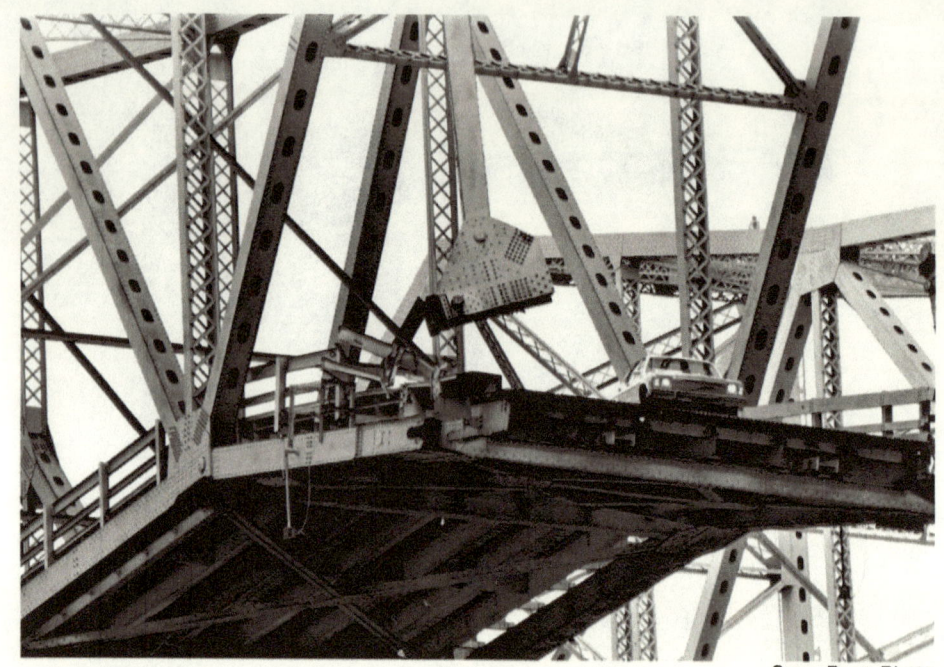

Gene Page Photo

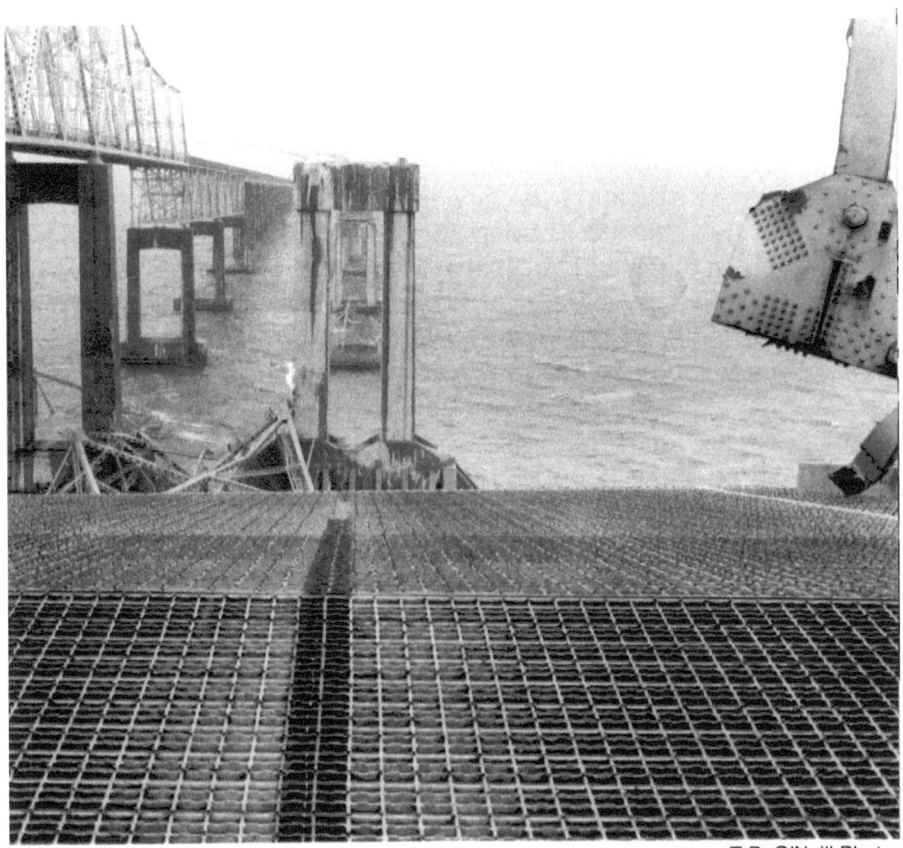

T.P. O'Neill Photo

Meanwhile, v Butterfield is coming up the incline. He Is moving so slowly his car begins to stall. Butterfield downshifts and gains speed. He sees the Chevy and sees Albritton sitting behind the wheel waving madly.

Butterfield starts to gain more speed and is preparing to pass the Chevy. "I am going to be late for school," he thinks. Butterfield recognizes the Chevy. It passed him minutes ago. Maybe the poor guy ran out of gas. In a mind's flash Butterfield recalls a sermon he heard in church, of how we are our brother's keeper. Butterfield pulls 15 yards ahead of the blue car and backs up. He gets out of the car and runs back to Albritton.

"What's the problem?"

"The bridge collapsed," Albritton says. *"Are you serious?"*

"I just saw a bus and two cars go past and I don't know how many more!"

Butterfield runs down the incline towards St. Petersburg, flailing his arms wildly. He stops one car, then another. He passes the news and the motorists stop dead in their tracks.

§ § § §

Wesley MacIntire's pickup truck is sinking to the bottom of the bay. The 56-year-old mechanic forces open the door and pushes himself free. He starts swimming to the surface. It is a long way up. There is blood coming from a gash on his head. He is swallowing water as he struggles for the surface. Exhausted, he grasps a piece of steel girder and holds on. The water churns around him. He vomits saltwater.

He looks skyward and sees the headlights of Hornbuckle' s Buick shining into the void below. It is quiet. There are no screams for help. A short distance away the *Summit Venture* sits motionlessly. MacIntire is dazed, unable to decide what to do. Should he swim for shore or to another section of bridge? The *Summit Venture*, its nose stuck under the far span, begins to move. MacIntire fights to clear his head. He yells. Someone from the *Summit Venture* throws out a lifeline. MacIntire swims to it and takes hold. He tries to pull himself up the rope ladder, but it is slippery. "Hold on!" the crew on deck shouts. They pull MacIntire up the face of the ship and onto the deck.

John Lerro is in the pilothouse on the radio to the Coast Guard.

Lerro:	"Mayday, Coast Guard, Mayday, Bridge crossing is down."
Lerro:	"Mayday, Mayday, Mayday, Coast Guard. Mayday, Mayday, Mayday, Coast Guard."
Coast Guard:	"Vessel calling Mayday. Vessel in distress. This is United States Coast Guard, St. Petersburg, Florida. Request your position, nature of distress, and number of persons on board. Over."
Lerro:	"This is — all the emergency — all the emergency equipment — out to the Skyway Bridge. Vessel just hit Skyway Bridge. The Skyway Bridge went down. Get all the emergency equipment out to the Skyway Bridge. The Skyway Bridge is down. This is Mayday. Emergency situation. Stop the traffic on that Skyway Bridge!"
Coast Guard:	"This is Coast Guard, St. Petersburg, roger. What size is the vessel that hit the bridge? Over."
Lerro:	(Garble traffic) "Special. Stop the traffic on the Skyway Bridge. There is some people in the water. Get some emergency equipment out to the Skyway Bridge now."
Coast Guard:	"This is the Coast Guard St. Petersburg, roger. What vessel are you on? Over."
Lerro:	"The *Summit Venture,* the *Summit Venture.*"
Coast Guard:	"*Summit Venture,* Coast Guard St. Petersburg, roger. What size is your vessel, and can you assist? Over."
Lerro:	"Cannot assist. We are six hundred and six feet long, light in ballast. We cannot assist. We hit an abutment. Stop all the traffic on the bridge, send some vessels out here to render assistance. People are (garbled) in the water."

28

By now the squall that engulfed the *Summit Venture* has raced onward. It swept across the bay east of the fallen Sunshine Skyway and focuses its fury on the *Pure Oil*, now within two miles east of the bridge. The rain is coming down in horizontal sheets, riding the wind, pouring into the pilothouse of the *Pure Oil*. John Schiffmacher of the Tampa Bay Pilots' Association looks at the *Pure Oil's* radar screen. It is as blank as the blackness of the storm that swallows the 505-foot tanker.

Schiffmacher orders a turn to starboard and the tanker begins turning clockwise out of the westbound channel. The turn to the right is made easier by the wind pressing against the vessel's port bow. As Schiffmacher prepares to drop anchor he watches the storm start to disappear as quickly as it appeared. "Maybe we'll get lucky and can just make a slow circle here and not have to anchor," he tells the captain of the ship.

Then they hear John Lerro's voice over the marine radio: **"Mayday, Coast Guard, Mayday, Mayday. Bridge crossing Is down..."**

The storm is gone, the sky is clear, and in the distance, John Schiffmacher witnesses the incredible: A quarter mile of the south bound span has disappeared.

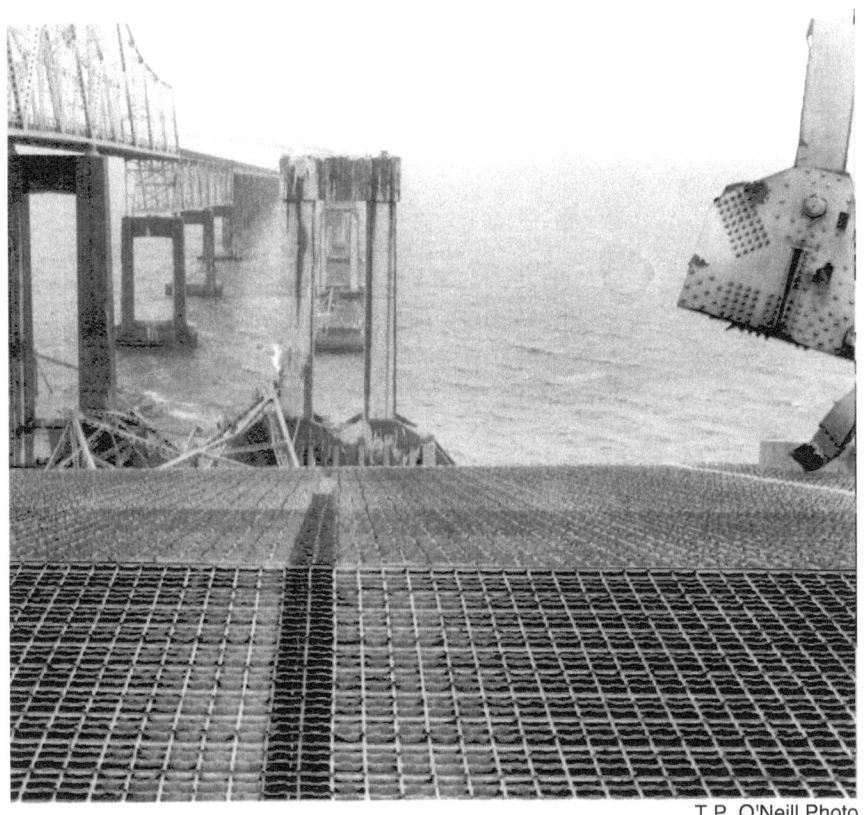

T.P. O'Neill Photo

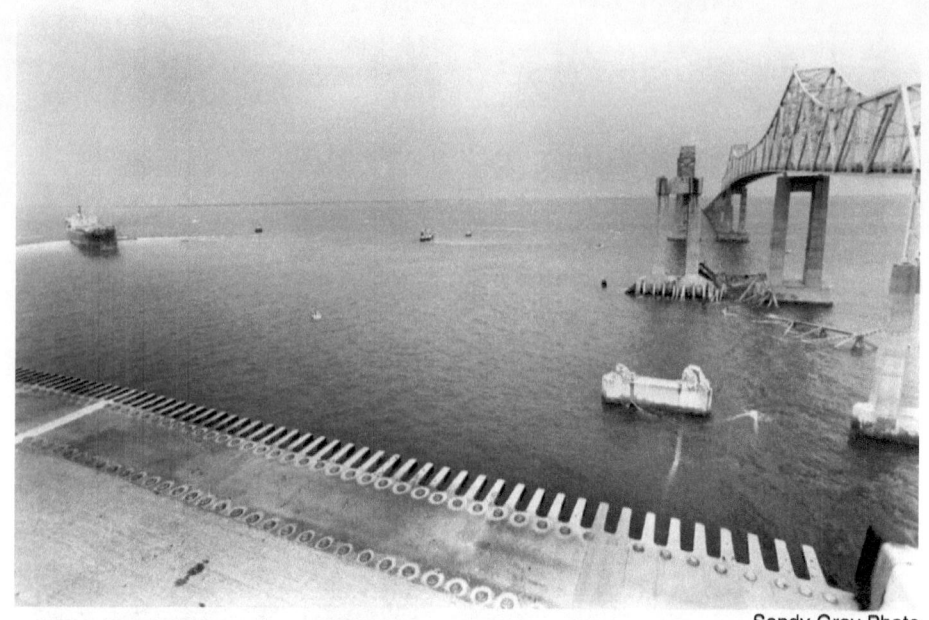

Sandy Gray Photo

From beneath a heap of roadway on the bow of the *Summit Venture* Sit Hau Po emerges. He crawls on his hands and knees. His head swims and terror is etched on his face. His muscles twitch uncontrollably. Miraculously, he is physically unscathed. When the bridge started falling, he dashed down and hid between two pieces of equipment on the ship's bow. Po surveys the debris and realizes he is lucky to be alive. About 30 yards of roadway lie across the bow and extend over both sides. It rests atop the winches used to control the forward anchors.

The two lanes of traffic make a roof over Po's hiding place. It is incredible the road remains intact. If it had not, Po would now be crushed beneath the rubble. The steel reinforcing rods under the pavement stop the roadway from crumbling. Near the road's black and white centerline, a loading arm on the *Summit Venture's* bow pierces the pavement like a spike through a piece of paper. The yellow sidelines of the road show through the twisted jagged steel girders that tumbled down from the canopied superstructure. One guardrail remains attached.

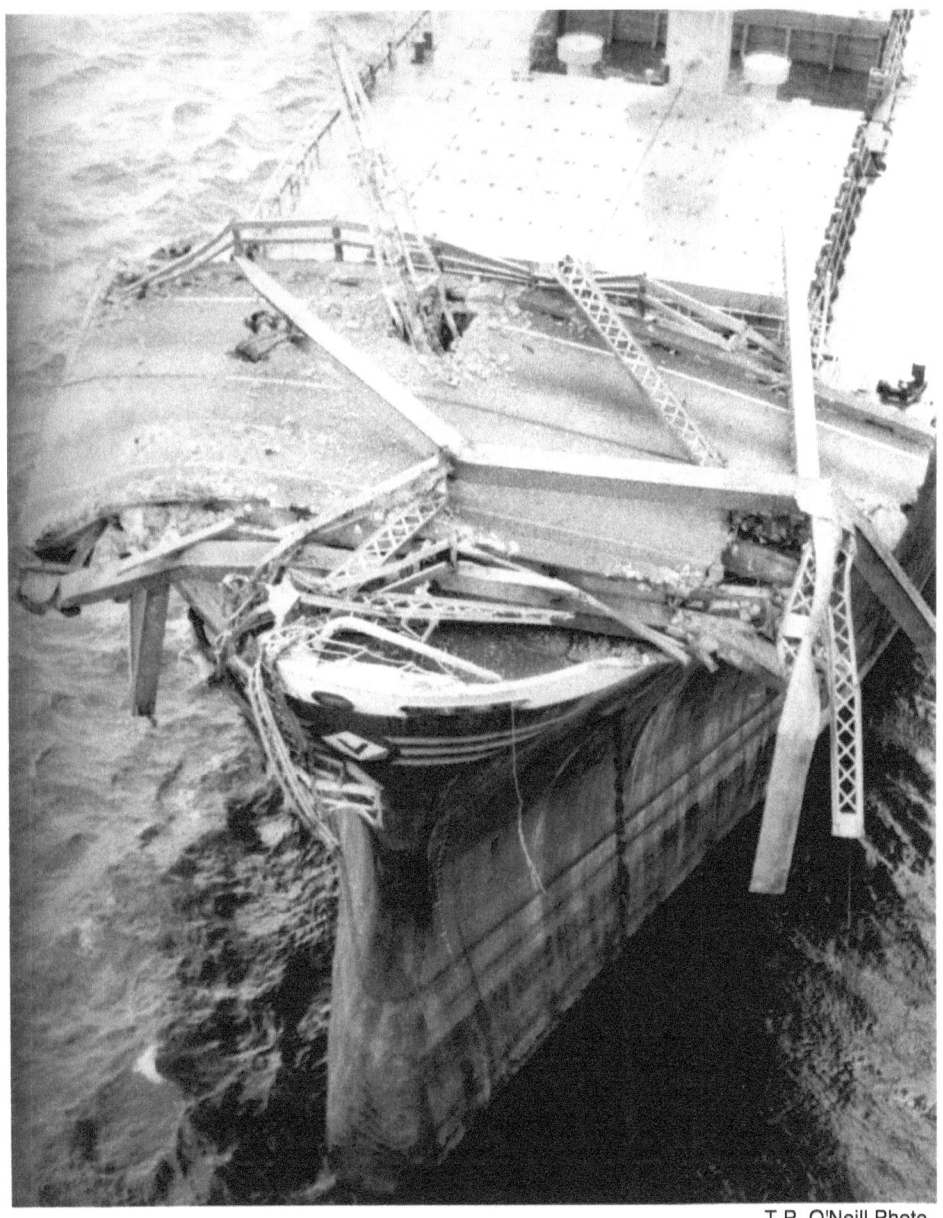

Florida Highway Patrolman Leroy McIntosh notices traffic slowing up ahead on the bridge. He just finished investigating a minor accident. McIntosh moves out quickly and threads his cruiser through the obstacle course of cars until he gets to the top.

Then McIntosh spots a group of men rushing toward him. It is Hornbuckle and his passengers, who minutes before bailed out of their car and crawled and slipped up the slick metal grating that now hangs over the bay. They wave frantically and their expressions tell the trooper something is seriously wrong.

McIntosh stops his cruiser and the men run up. He cannot believe what he is hearing. He hikes to the top and looks over the ragged edge. In the distance he can see the other side of the bridge. Below sits the *Summit Venture* and its cluttered bow. An entire set of concrete support pilings is gone. Portions of the super structure stick out of the water. The steel girders look like the pieces of a child's erector set. Through the metal grid under his feet McIntosh sees the Greyhound bus. It is upside down and its wheels are a few feet below the surface. McIntosh has never seen anything like this, not even as a soldier in Vietnam. He goes to his cruiser to radio for help.

Meanwhile, Richard Hornbuckle creeps down the lip of metal grating toward his car. All four doors are open, and it appears the wind Is grabbing them, causing the car to inch even further down the broken piece of bridge. Hornbuckle thinks the car might sail over the edge and into the bay. He removes the keys from the ignition and begins shutting the doors. He is careful not to look down. He can hear people yelling at him. Hornbuckle must do only one more thing. The clubs – they are in the trunk and he has a golfing date tomorrow.

His friends, the trooper, spectators, they are all yelling – "Get out of there!" Hornbuckle heeds their warnings and works his way back to firm footing.

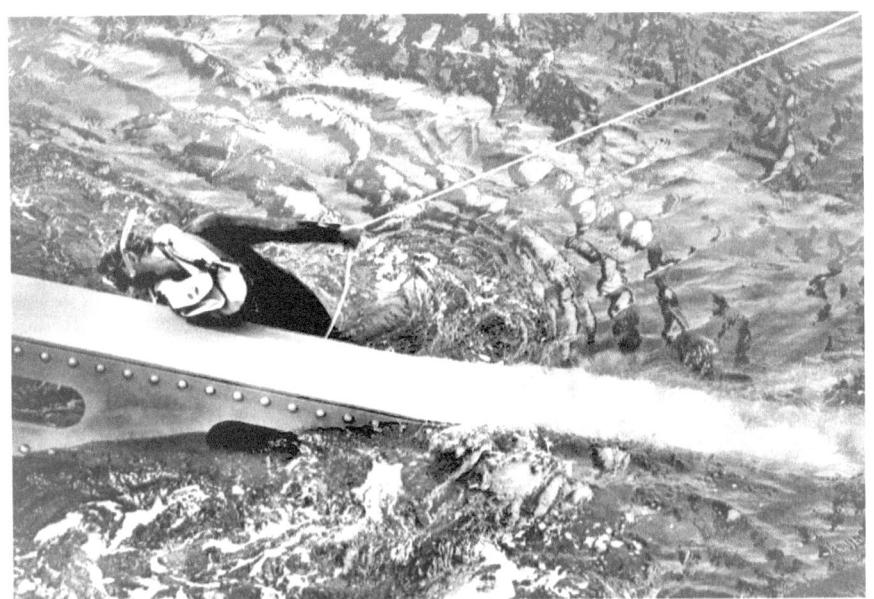

Phil Skinner Photo

Chapter 3
Search & Rescue

Two hours after the Skyway fell the first bloody body surfaces. A rescue diver grips the stark white arm of a shirtless man. The current whips his body around like a limp rag doll.

Black-clad divers stand on the belly of the bus with the bay lapping at their waists. Bubbles of diesel fuel break the surface and are carried away by the current. A diver enters the open door of the Greyhound. There are rumors there may be an air bubble in the bus. It is possible people are still alive in there. The diver emerges, pulling a body behind him. It's a woman. For some odd reason she is without a blouse. The whiteness of her brassiere stands out boldly against the green-gray bay.

An inspection of the exterior of the bus proves there is no chance for survivors. Its roof has been sheared away. It becomes obvious now: The bus drove off the end of the bridge and fell nose first into the bay. The massive steel girders tore the roof off all the way down to the windows. No human being could have survived the impact. The tangle of girders stops the Greyhound from sinking.

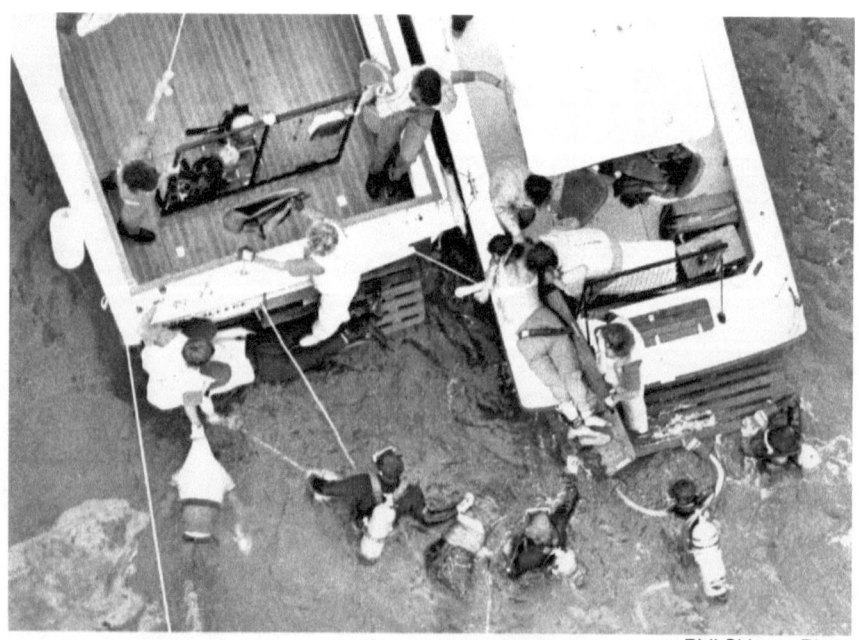

Phil Skinner Photo

35

Divers are finding more cars in the jungle of metal and concrete below the surface. By the way the cars are bunched – tangled and twisted in the mass of girders – it is apparent they followed one another off the end of the bridge. So far, three cars have been spotted – some of them with their occupants trapped inside. It looks like a colossal underwater freeway crash. There is no telling how many more vehicles are down there. It is dark down there and the current makes the diver's job treacherous. Pieces of debris fall from the bridge occasionally. There is the chance the girders will shift beneath the surface. The bloody mess is starting to attract sharks. Some divers are ordered from the water. Enough people have lost their lives today, authorities reason. Other divers stay on, however. There is work to be done.

More bodies trapped inside the Greyhound begin to surface – a silver-haired woman in a pink pants suit, a muscular young black man, a black woman in jeans. Luggage and purses float everywhere. Divers pull the bodies to rescue boats and struggle to slide their lifeless forms into body bags. But the bay is too rough as the weather again turns nasty. They haul the bodies aboard and pile them face down on top of one another in the bow of the boat. A pool of bloody water collects beneath them.

Tugs are pushing the *Summit Venture* away from the bridge. It is relocated 500 yards to the west, near where the Blackthorn once sank to the bottom. The heap of girders and roadway hangs across its nose like tinsel on a Christmas tree. The Coast Guard has taken command of the ship. To the east, the *Pure Oil* sits at anchor.

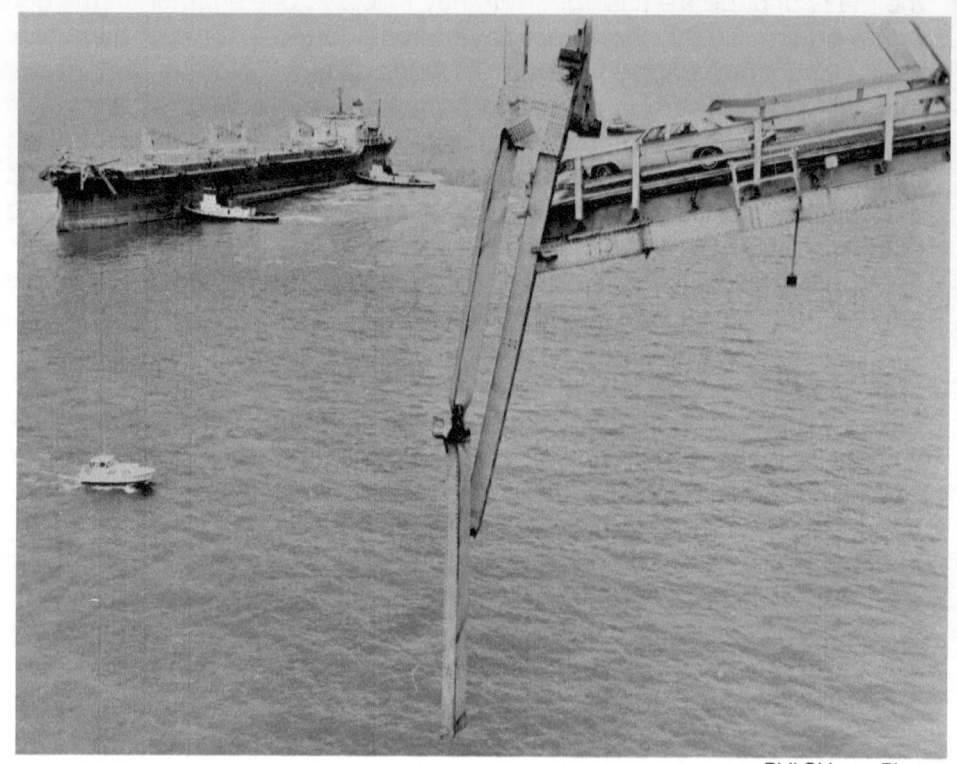

Phil Skinner Photo

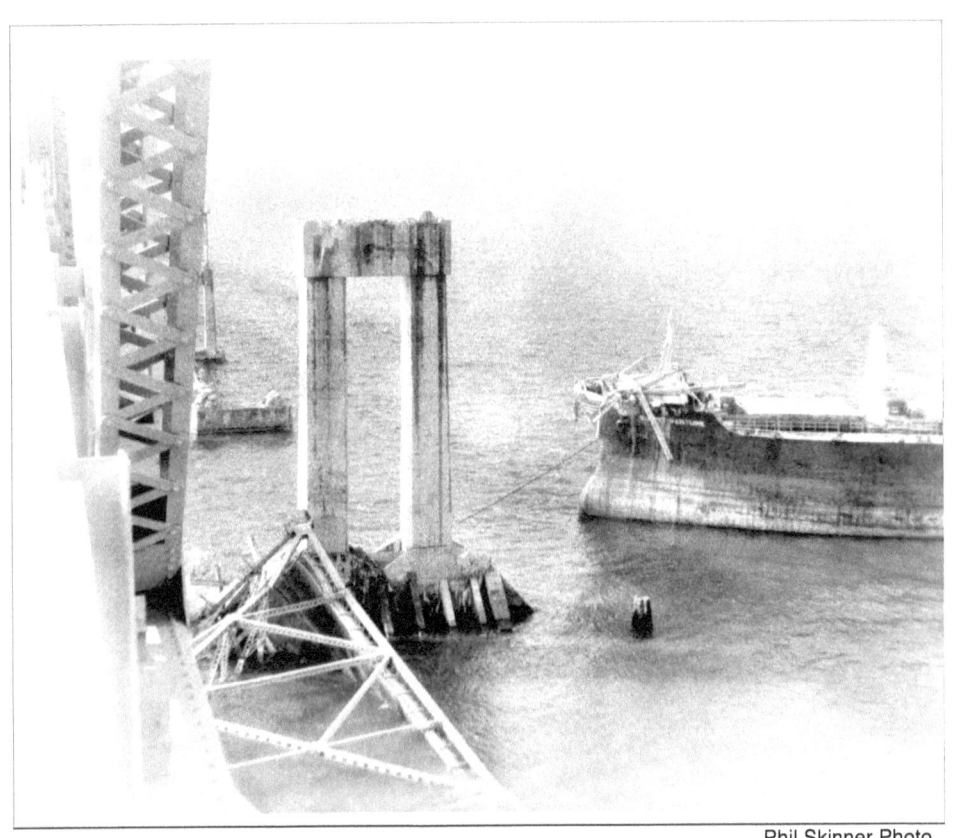

Phil Skinner Photo

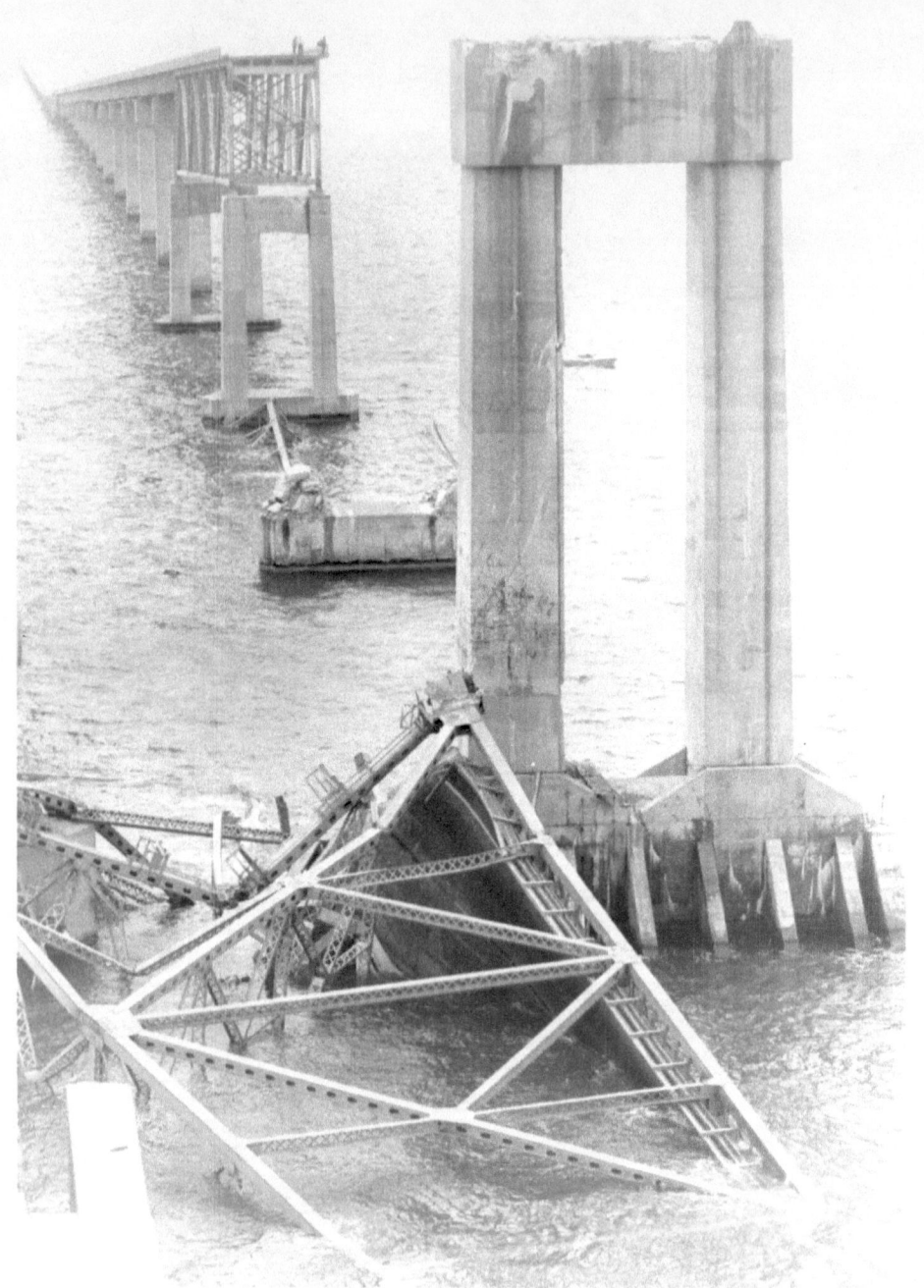

Phil Skinner Photo

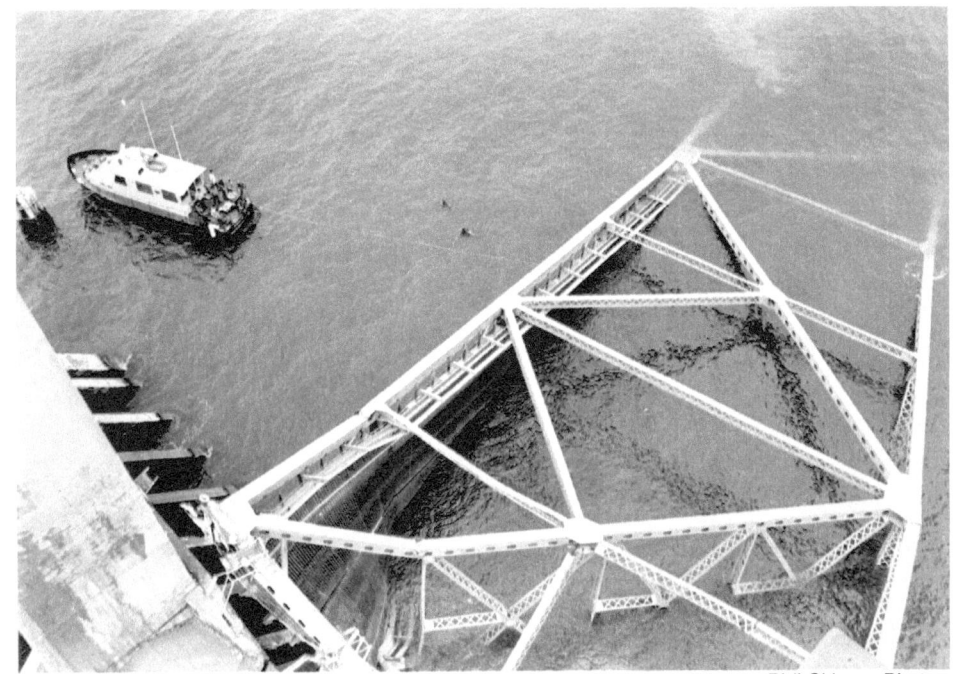
Phil Skinner Photo

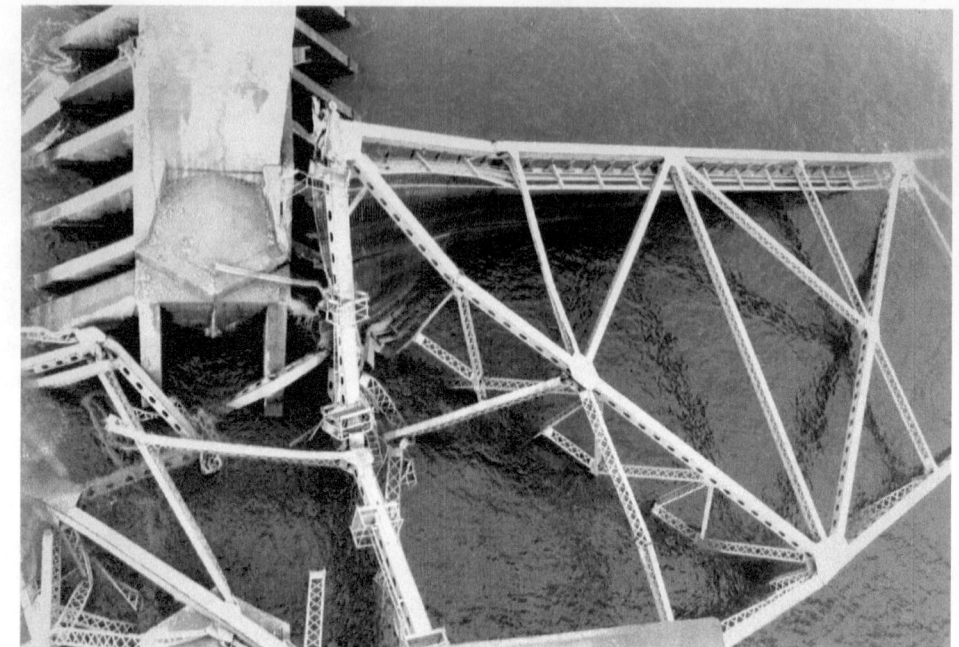

Phil Skinner Photo

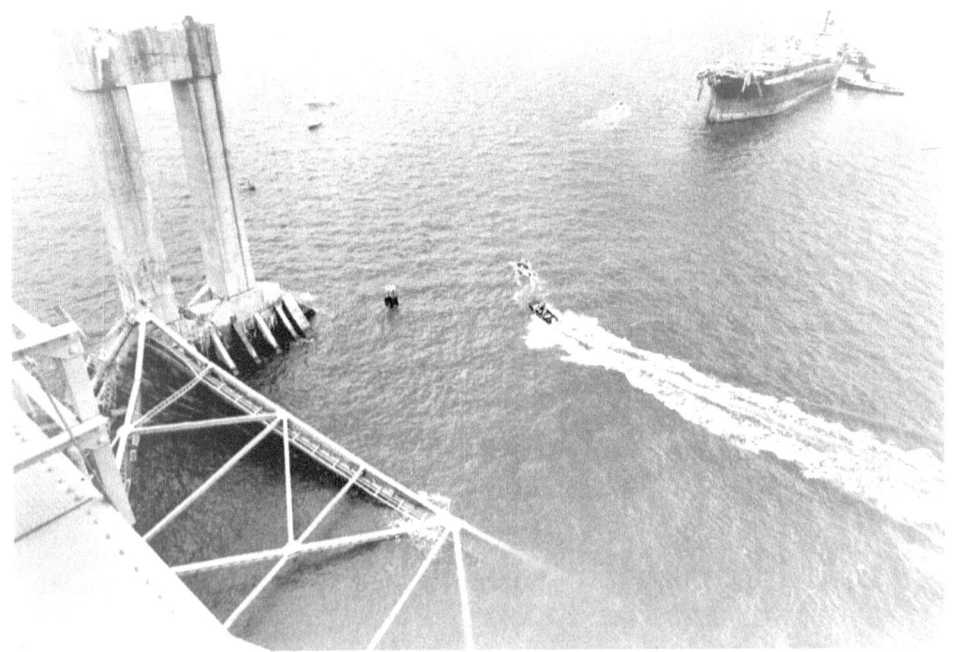

Phil Skinner Photo

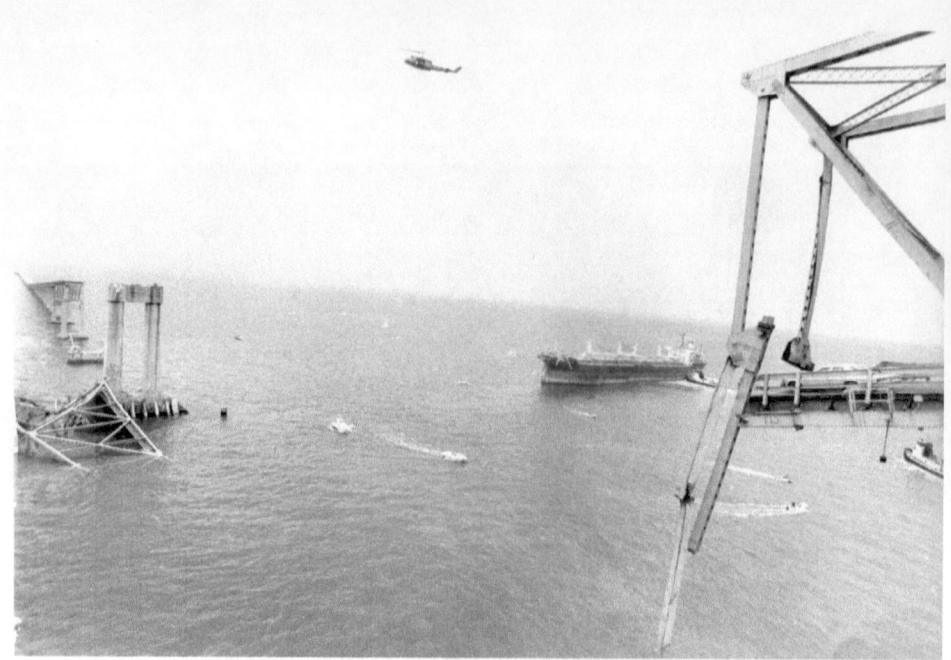

At the Greyhound station in Sarasota a woman with a brown shag haircut, white-knit top, jeans and white shoes waits impatiently. Nearby a tall blond young man sits at one of those "TV" chairs.
The TV flashes aerial views of the Sunshine Skyway and a voice intones the tragic details.

"They ought to take the captain of the ship and hang him," the young man says, shaking his head in disgust.
"What bus went off the bridge?" the woman asks.
"They say it was Trailways," he replies.
"Well, we're safe," she says.

At 10:30 a.m. a man in a green khaki uniform enters the station, walks to the ticket counter and asks the clerk if he has heard anything about the 7:05 out of St. Petersburg. The clerk shakes his head. Negative.

The woman catches up with the man in the green khaki uniform as he walks away. *"Where is the Greyhound bus?"* she asks.
"In the bay."
Her jaw goes slack. She moves to the ticket counter. *"What's this I hear about a bus in the bay?"*
"I don't know," says the clerk. *"Did you know someone on the bus?"*
"My husband." Then Julie Russell turns and walks away.

Chapter 4
Makeshift Morgue

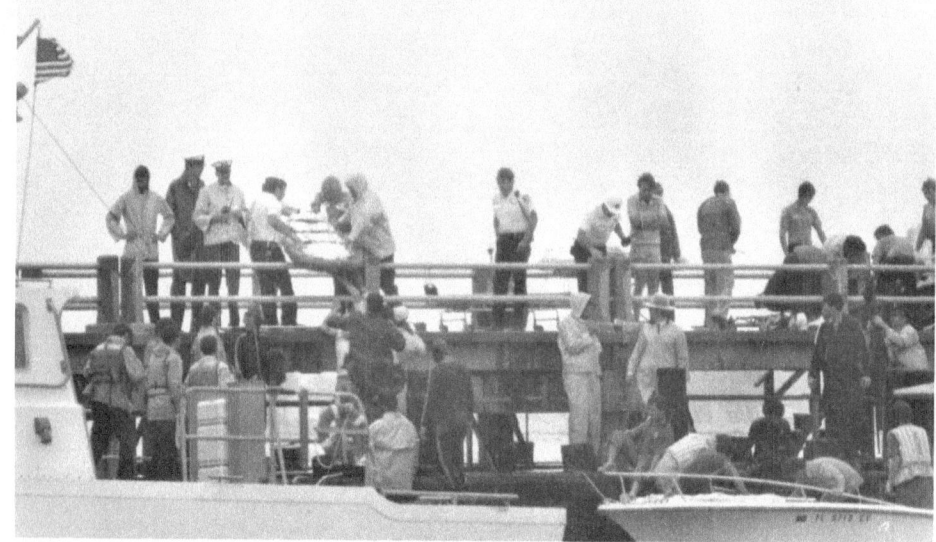

The first rescue boat loaded with corpses moves out towards Mullet Key, three miles to the northwest. Fort DeSoto Park on the key has been established as the command post and the makeshift morgue. Dozens of paramedics, ambulance drivers, lawmen and clergy mill about. So do cameramen and reporters. The story of the Skyway has gone national and the media is turning out in force. There is no telling how many people are in the bay or how big this story will break. It could become the world's worst bridge disaster. The Tampa Bay area alone has eight daily newspapers, four TV network affiliates, and numerous radio stations. All are staffed by young aggressive professionals out to make a name for themselves in one of the nation's most lucrative and competitive media markets.

Peter B. Gallagher of the St. Petersburg Times is there. Well-known for his offbeat brand of journalism, Gallagher captured the mood better than anyone else when he filed this report:

~~~

MULLET KEY - The first four bodies came in on three stretchers. They were easy to find, just floating away from the killer bridge. *Hey, man, we did this same thing a couple months ago, you know*. Rescue divers hoisted the four onto cutters and then came in for coffee, sick of pulling bodies out of the water. *It's a waste. That bridge has taken a damn lot of human life since it's been up*. Everyone at the command post agrees. The bridge killed them.

Two Jane Does and a John were dropped into body bags by morgue workers. One other, smaller, was swaddled in a white cloth. *I'll tell you right now we're going to run out of bags on this one. That bus could have 75 people on it.* The four victims were lifted, passed, carried up, passed and softly dropped onto the Mullet Key Pier. *Jesus Christ, we ought to build a morgue right out here. Wasn't the Blackthorn, what, two, three months ago?*

They were "processed." Tagged John or Jane. Then morgue men dropped them on rolling stretchers. Then a procession began – from gray sea to gray Ford morgue transport van. The crowd went tight-lipped.
At the van, a morgue man lays down a rule: "Take your pictures but none inside the van. Please. We aren't using stretches in there, and it won't look good. This doesn't happen every day, you know." Two bodies are slid inside. The small white bundle is taken from atop the third body. "A baby," the morgue man curses.

What? A construction worker with tattoos all over his arms wants to know. "A baby." *Jee-sus. This is unbelievable.* It is. At sea, a dead man hangs over the stern of a boat and a pelican swoops toward him. Rescue divers keep shooing it away; on land, body No. 7 is stacked into the van while the men pushing No. 8 make a U-turn and return to the pier. *What the hell?* "Did somebody make a mistake? Is it still alive?" a television man surmises. The TV crew runs after it.

"Not processed yet, that's all," sneers a morgue man. "Forgot to tag it John or Jane, that's all." A worker trying to straighten the bodies trips and falls on Number 3 and 4. Christ, *we're going to have to start alternating them feet and head.* The next van is opened. More bodies slide in.

No. 13 is a black man in tennis shoes. No. 14 is barefooted. A Catholic priest approaches a morgue man. "Can I...?" Father Brian Kilbride carries a holy water bottle and purple Extreme Unction stole. "Father, can we wait? There's too many cameras here. You know?"

Another front is moving in. Rain soaks the scene. What is left of the Skyway Bridge disappears from the horizon. No. 15 is a thin white woman. No. 16 is a large white man. By 11:30, eight Johns, eight Janes and the baby have come in. A TV reporter muses: *Aren't there any relatives out here wondering where their sister or son is or something?*

The next stretcher has no body bag. Breathing human being Wesley MacIntire, elbow in the air, head wrapped in gauze, sole survivor of this tragedy. They slide him into an ambulance and head for St. Anthony's hospital. *Where they going with him?* A group of reporters runs up. "Bayfront Medical Center," someone lies. A swarm takes off for the phones. Someone laughs.

During the confusion, Father Kilbride walks to the side of one van. A morgue man in a yellow raincoat slides open the side door. The priest throws the purple stole around his neck, mumbles and casts holy water upon the body bags and soaked sheets. He repeats the ceremony in the next van. The two vans leave for the coroner's office.

"A tragedy," The priest has an Irish brogue. "All people setting out for a day's journey, suddenly called to their eternal reward. God bless them. Oh, God bless them."

Two detectives walk off the pier carrying a bulging brown suitcase and a small white handbag that says *Phyllis Hudson* on the name tag. *What is that?* A newswoman sticks her tape recorder forward. "What does it look like?" snarls the detective. "Oh my God," exclaims Kris Rebillot of Channel 8. "There's not a baby in there, is there?" The detective looks skyward in disgust.

Body 18 comes in at 1:15 p.m. A John. The crowd rushes to the third gray van. Photographers press forward. "Gentlemen, some moderation, please," pleads a morgue man. There is blood on the stretcher. "A lot of them had bad head wounds," says the morgue man. "The others had some pretty horrible expressions on their faces. But I'm not supposed to tell you that."

Two elderly people run stumbling forward and begin firing questions at Rabbi David Susskind (who is out here "Because I heard there were Jewish victims," he says.)

"I just want to know what color the cars were," says Jule Berger, a St. Petersburg Beach retiree. "They left this morning at seven to go to Bradenton and they haven't called or anything. That's not like them. I don't know. I don't know. I just want to know the colors..."

A sad mystery unfolds. *Everyone guesses the ending.* Harry and Hildred Dietch left St. Petersburg Beach Friday morning at 7. Harry is a 70-year-old shoe salesman who had an appointment in Palmetto. Hildred is an attractive woman in her 70s who always has her hair done at the same salon in Bradenton.

"These are our good friends. They are punctual people," says Mrs. Berger. "Their children are coming in from Mississippi at l:00 p.m. Her only daughter is flying into Tampa for Mother's Day. They would have surely called."

The Bergers stumble off through the crowd. *What to do? Who to ask? What color?* "We have to assume the worst," whispers Rabbi Susskind. "I knew the people. They were not the type to be inhibited by weather. They would've called."

Suddenly the crowd turns back to the pier. Three stretchers are coming off. *Empty.* The crowd stands and looks anyway. "The search is being suspended for a while until the weather breaks," says Hillsborough County Sheriff Walter Heinrich.

He gazes out toward the killer bridge: "Everybody's always talked about this happening. I admit I thought about it every time I went over it." Every head in earshot of his statement begins shaking hell yes.

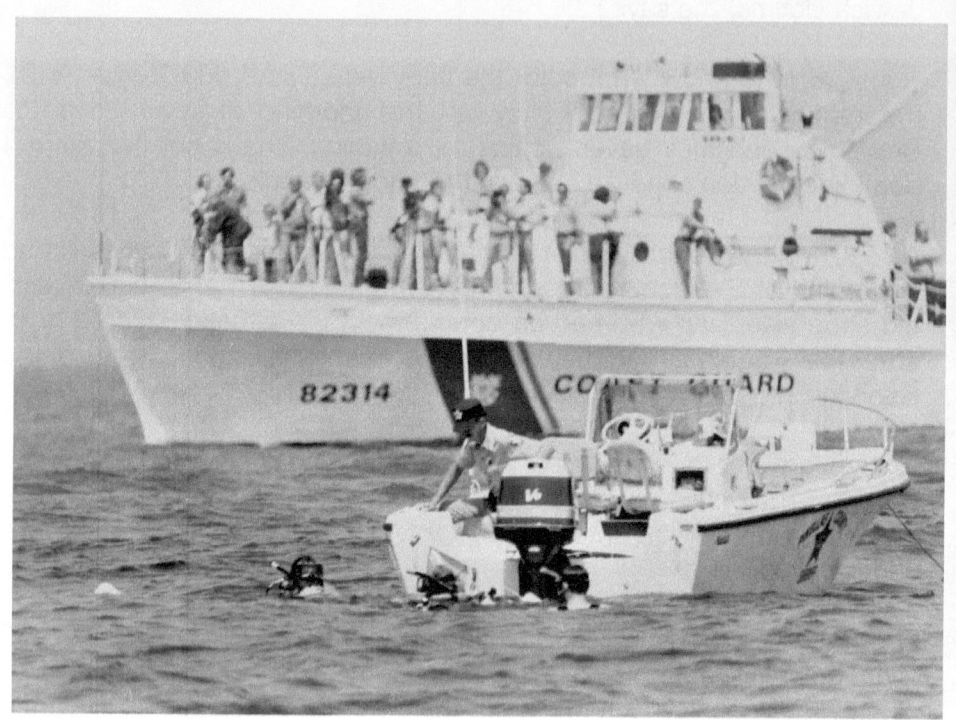

Gene Page Photo

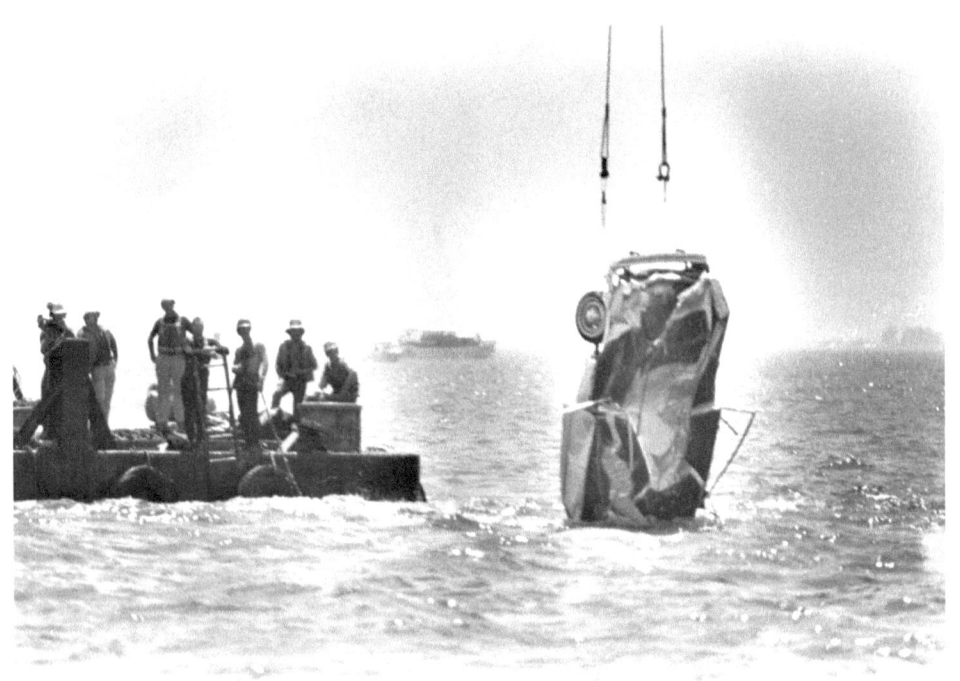

Gene Page Photo

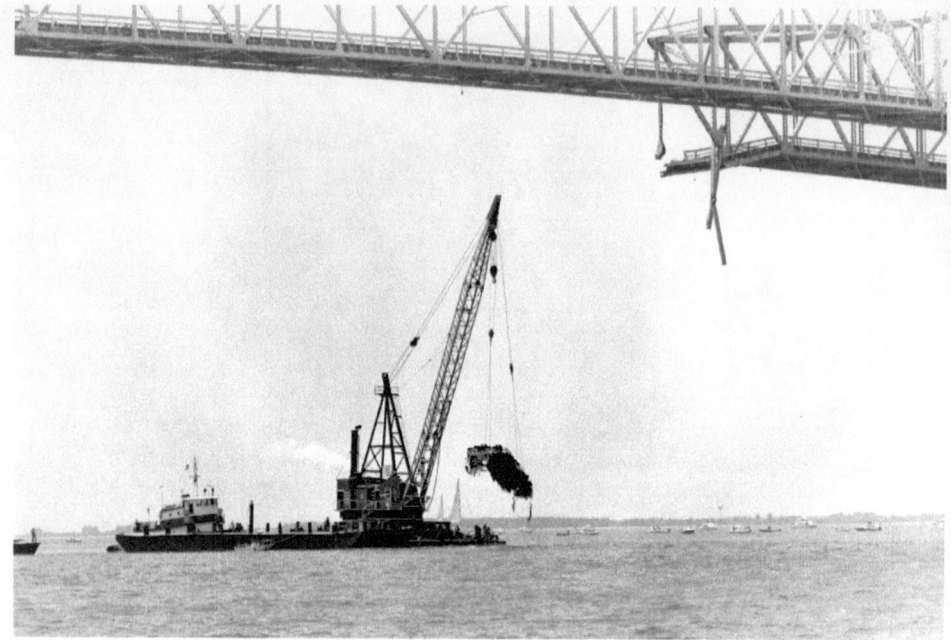

Gene Page Photo

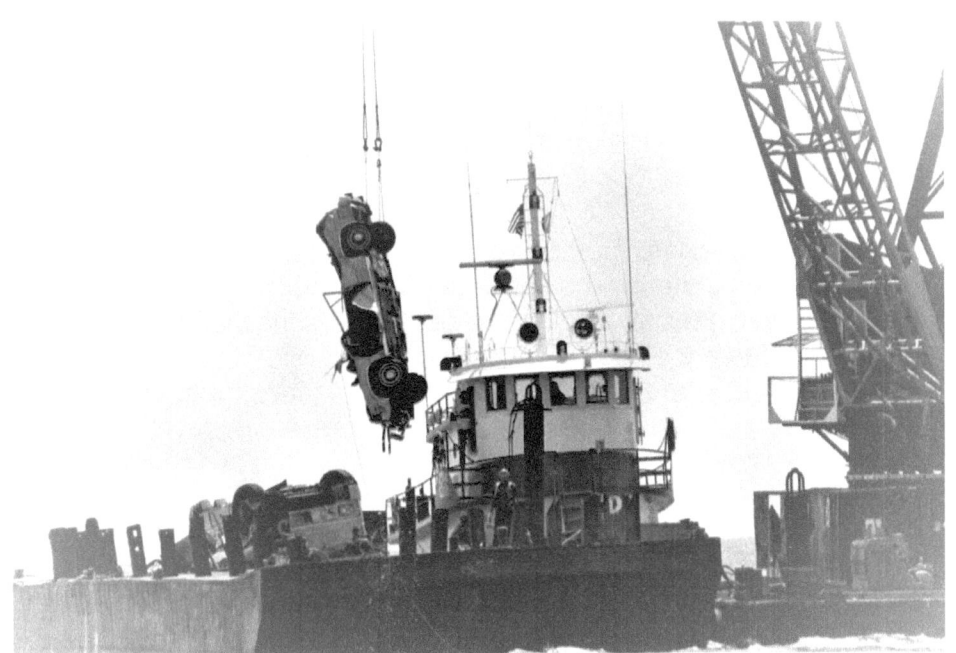

Authorities seal the morgue in Tampa and the Hillsborough County medical examiner goes to work. Autopsies show the victims died from lacerated lungs, smashed skulls and crushed chests. The fright of falling 15 stories into the bay seems enough to scare a person to death. Some corpses are so disfigured, dental and blood records may be necessary to make identifications.

Detectives are making some progress sifting through the personal items found at the scene. They are sorting through two stretchers loaded with suitcases, purses, shaving kits, shoes, medicine vials, deodorants and a variety of personal effects. The detectives are searching for clues that might reveal the identity of the dead. No one asks your name or keeps a passenger log when you buy a bus ticket. But already the personal effects have yielded the identities of several passengers.

The Coast Guard is conducting an intense surface search for survivors. A spokesman promises the search will continue through Friday night, then adds an ominous footnote: "The Coast Guard is in the business of searching for survivors – not bodies. When we feel there is no possibility for life, we will cancel the search and move to where we are needed for other rescue efforts."

With each passing hour it becomes more obvious only Wesley MacIntire survived. He is in the hospital with a sprained neck, water in his lungs and a cut on his head. "It's miraculous, absolutely miraculous he survived," says MacIntire's physician. "His injuries are on the level of a common automobile accident."

MacIntire Is rolled into the corridor of the hospital. His head is swaddled in a big white bandage. The cameras roll; strobe lights explode like it is the 4th of July. Wesley MacIntire, a 56-year-old mechanic, is an instant celebrity. He tells the pack of reporters the details of his ordeal. "How do you feel?" the reporters ask. "I'm sore all over, that's for sure."

Divers again are in the water. A new rumor is afloat. A bus of migrant farm workers crossed the Skyway Friday morning; the bus has not arrived at its destination. Could it be wrapped in the web of steel beneath the bridge?

Overhead a helicopter circles. It carries U.S. Sen. Richard Stone, the Miami Democrat who was witnessing the Cuban refugee evacuation in Key West when word of the Skyway arrived. A shaken Stone tells reporters: "I feel horrible I've been over that span before and wondered what would happen if a ship hit it. It looks like something out of one of those disaster movies like the Towering Inferno."

Curiosity seekers are starting to pour into the area. It is difficult to fathom how this could happen. People must see it to believe it. It is like nuclear war: so abhorrent that it is unreal in the minds of men. But it happened. The proof is in the middle of the bay. The Skyway looks like it has been bombed.

The Coast Guard and its auxiliary circle the area with sentry boats to ward off curiosity seekers. The pleasure crafts give up after a while and move off. O'Neill's Skyway Boat Basin is beginning to swell with boaters. Motorists are stopping at the popular roadside establishment to gawk at the bridge in the distance. It's a rerun of the scene five months earlier, when the Capricorn and Blackthorn collided.

People are standing in small groups, swigging beer, discussing the latest rumors, trying to imagine the terror of driving off the end of the bridge, hurtling through space, dropping down, waiting out those last seconds.

53

A constant theme runs through the conversations. The Skyway must be cursed. It's got to be. Three times in four months ships have struck the bridge. Something like this was bound to happen. Someone should have taken the proper precautions. Who's at fault? The pilot? Or was it an act of God

A commercial fisherman tells of the time he was anchored beneath the bridge and all of a sudden – splash – a leaper. He pulls the body from the water. "He died on the bow of my boat," the fisherman tells his audience.

One story sparks another. They are like children telling ghost stories before bedtime. Another fisherman steps forward and offers an explanation. During construction of the Skyway a worker fell into wet cement. Buried alive, his body remains a part of the bridge. What other explanation can there be for today's cursed events?

The authorities refuse to list the names of the dead who have been identified. The next of kin must be notified first. Some have received the sad news already.

Jim Pryor's family knows. The El Camino was spotted in the wreckage; a body was pinned behind the wheel. Pryor's attaché case was found floating in the water.

Julie Russell told authorities about the tattoo on Mel's shoulder. It was there, just as she described it.

The body of the baby is that of Monisha McGarrah. Wanda McGarrah remains missing. No one has heard from Harry and Hildred Dietch. Their fate seems obvious.

The estimated number of dead is put at 32. Right now, eighteen bodies – 10 women, seven men and the baby – are in the morgue. Several cars are beneath the bay, some with more than one body inside. No one really knows how many perished. "The toll could go higher," says a Coast Guard spokesman. "Much higher."

The divers are frustrated in their attempts Saturday to bring up more bodies. They count nine corpses trapped in vehicles wrapped in the jungle of debris. But it is physically Impossible to remove the occupants.

"It's not just a matter of going in to get the victims out; some of them are twisted in the steel," explains Sheriff Heinrich. The divers are unprepared to pry through the maze of girders and into the crumpled vehicles. Commercial hardhat divers are needed. They can use underwater cutting torches and explosives. A barge-borne derrick is needed to pull the vehicles loose and haul them to the surface.

Strange things are happening beneath the bay. Probing into the dark depths under the bridge brings more mystery. The El Camino with the body pinned behind the wheel – it has disappeared now. And hundreds of yards south of the channel a new oil slick has appeared. It is different from the slicks coming from the cars. It resembles the slick from the Greyhound. Could there really be another bus down there? And what about this bumper found on the bottom? It is off a Volkswagen Rabbit? Only no one has spotted a Volkswagen in the wreckage.

"I'm not saying there aren't more cars down there," says Major Cal Henderson of the Hillsborough County Sheriff's Department. "We just don't know."

The sheriff's department puts the death toll at 30, based on the number of bodies recovered and what can be seen underwater. But there could be as many as 32, a spokesman concedes.

The Coast Guard revises its count from Friday. Thirty-one dead is more like it. One corpse must have been counted twice; a spokesman explains.

One thing is certain: no bodies are found Saturday.

Authorities finally release the list of known dead: Duane Adderly, 21, Miami; Michael J. Curtin, 43, Apollo Beach; Sharon Elaine Dixon, 22, Miami, Yvonne Johnson, 22, Miami; Louis Luca, 52, Birmingham, Alabama; Monisha McGarrah, six months, Tallahassee.

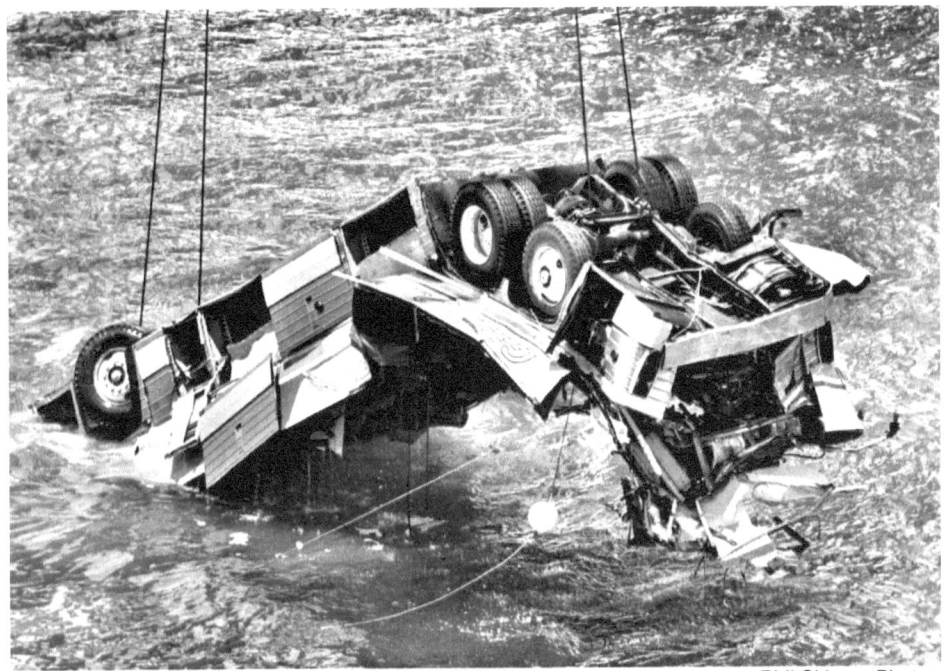

Phil Skinner Photo

Chapter 5
The Gawkers

Sunday blooms into one of those remarkable Florida Suncoast days. The foul weather is gone, and Tampa Bay once again turns into the land of sky and water. It's a great day for an outing, and the picnic areas on both sides of the Sunshine Skyway are filling quickly. Pack a lunch, grab the radio, a blanket and binoculars. Squeeze the family into the station wagon and make-off for the Skyway. They are going to raise the Greyhound bus and it's the best show in town. Don't forget the suntan oil.

Or get in a boat and sail up the shipping channel. You can sit in comfort, cooled by the sea breeze, and with the ghostly remains of the Skyway for a backdrop, watch the salvage operation. Fiddle with the radio and it is possible to monitor communication between the divers and salvage boats.

As the barge bearing the big derrick moves into the shadows of the Sunshine Skyway, dozens of pleasure crafts form a floating grandstand just outside the perimeter of the salvage site. And what is this steaming up? A cruise ship, the Captain Anderson, with at least 300 rubber-necked gawkers on board. The passengers jockey for position along the rail for the best view; the hard-hat divers descend to attend their grim business.

They explore the bus and radio to the surface, "It's broken in pieces...There are some bodies on the bus." They strain against the current of the shipping channel and work to secure cables around the axles. Mission accomplished.

The engines that power the derrick roar into high gear and suddenly the shiny silver metal of the Greyhound gleams in the sun. It hangs in the air, toy-like against the broken bridge, with water spewing forth from its battered sides. The roof is gone down to the windows and the sides with their familiar Greyhound logo stick out like stunted wings. The bus resembles a child's toy left in the driveway too long.

As the upside-down bus is pulled from the bay, two bodies are sucked free. The derrick lifts the bus high, swings it around, and dumps it with a thud on the deck of the barge. It Is 12:08 p.m. – 52 hours and 34 minutes after Mike Curtin and his 22 passengers plummeted 15 stories into the bay.

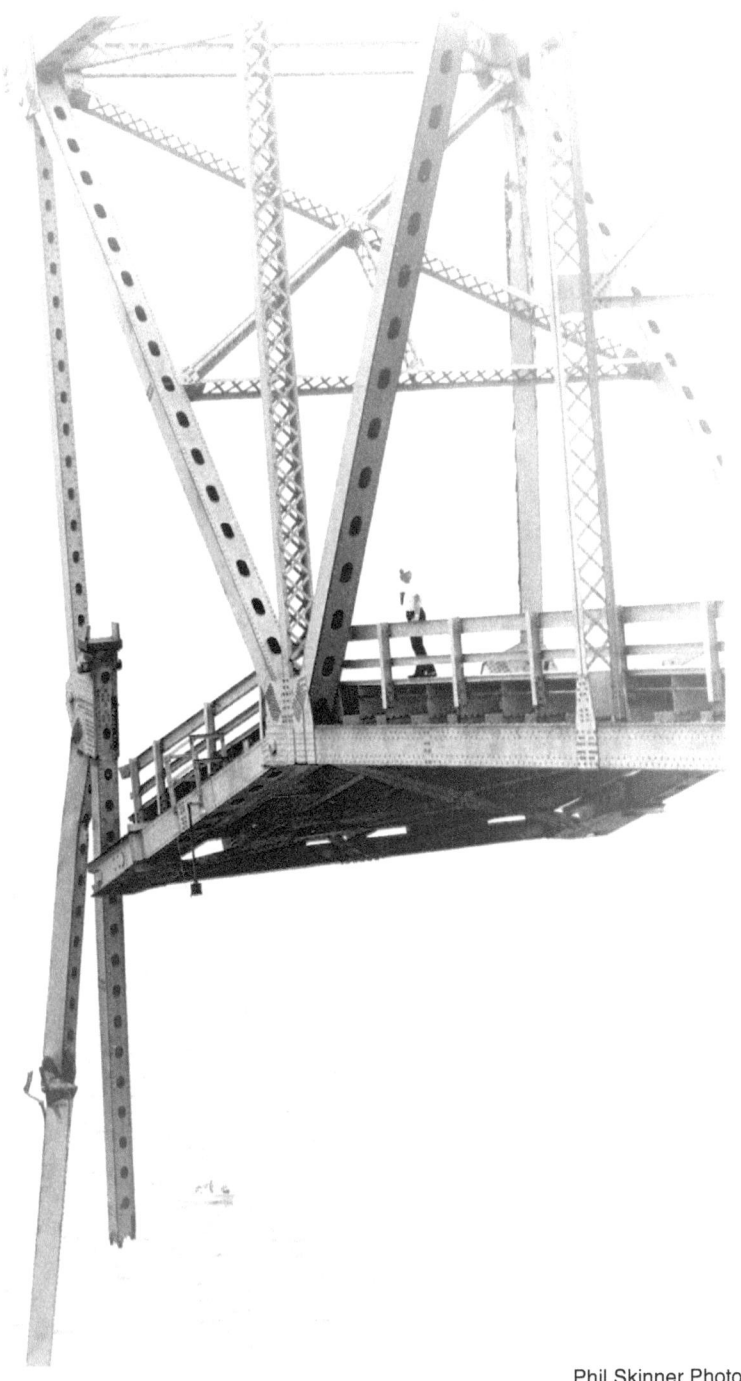

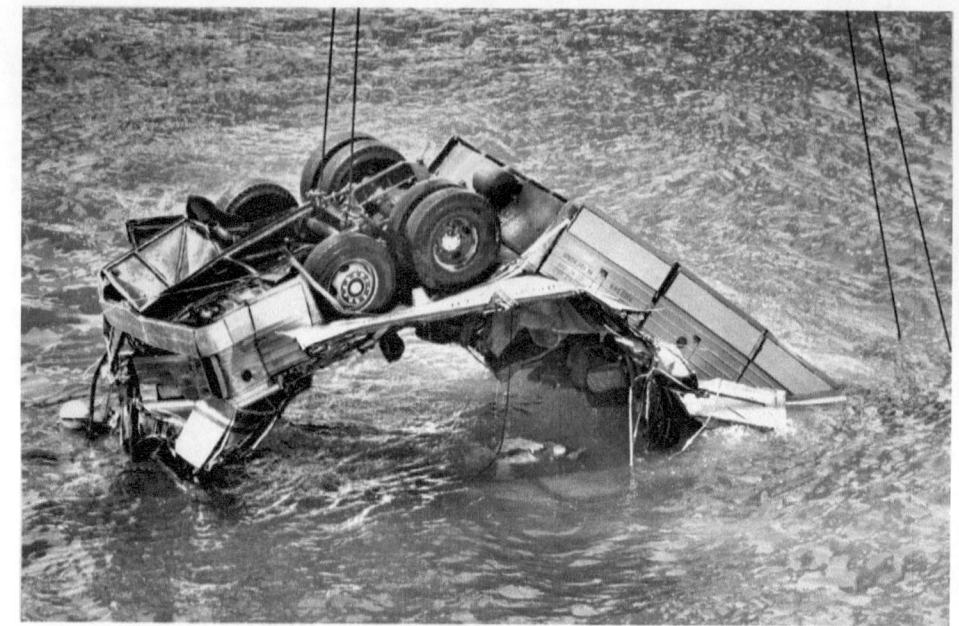

Phil Skinner Photo

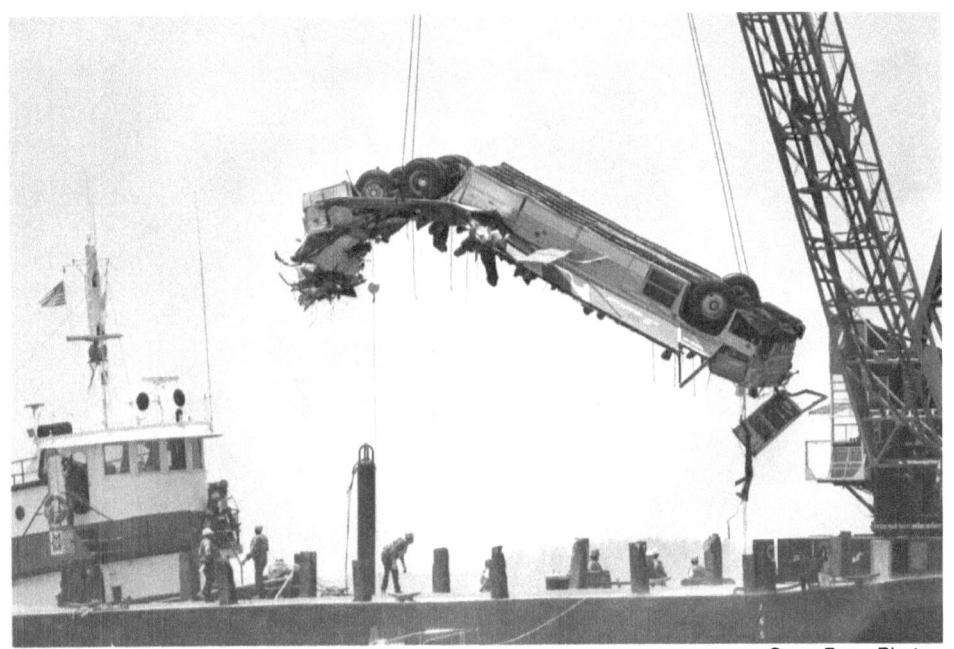

Gene Page Photo

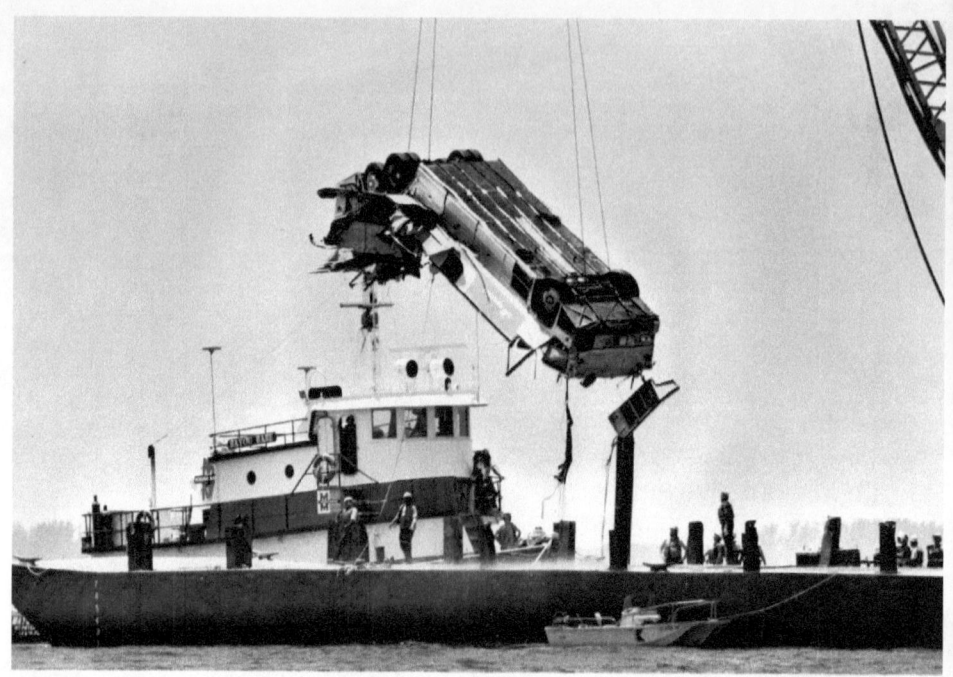

The divers repeat the procedure and up comes a 1980 blue Chevrolet Chevette. Inside are two bodies. A man and a woman – John Carlson, 47, of North Pinellas Park, and his 41-year-old wife Doris.

Then comes the 1973 Ford Torino, yellow and heavily damaged. Hildred and Harry Dietch never had a chance.

A man's body is found on the bottom of the bay, bringing Sunday's body count to seven, upping the number of bodies in the morgue to 25. With fair weather and good working conditions the body search might be finished by Monday. Unless, of course, the divers turn up that bus of migrant workers.

Meanwhile, the northbound lane of the Skyway has been restriped with a double-yellow no-passing line and traffic is beginning to move both ways. The northbound span suffered some structural damage, but the Florida Department of Transportation certifies it safe. Traffic is heavy, or so it seems, as cars crawl up the incline and onto the metal grating of the superstructure with its cage of steel girders. Toll-takers report a jovial mood among motorists. Some want to know why the toll is not half as much. After all, there is only half as much bridge to cross.

Four hundred fifty miles away in Montgomery, Alabama the heads of hundreds of students are bowed in silent prayer. They pray for the souls of former classmates Duane Adderly, Linda Daniels, Yvonne Johnson, Sharon Elaine Dixon and John Callaway. *May they rest in peace, amen.*

§ § § §

In Tampa, the sheriff's department announces it will investigate the ramming of the Skyway to learn if criminal charges should be brought against John Lerro, Capt. Hsiung Chu Lui, and those persons responsible for certifying the bridge safe.

Lerro's lawyer releases a statement: " ...the pilot respectfully declines to comment...since he has been advised by the United States Coast Guard that a Marine Board of Investigation will shortly be reconvened...It would be improper for Capt. Lerro to comment publicly."

But while Lerro refuses to talk to the public, the public is talking about Lerro. The newspapers, radio and TV are abuzz: The pilot of the *Summit Venture* has had seven previous accidents in 42 months of piloting on Tampa Bay. One mishap every six months. If he had been a motorist his license would have been yanked long ago, is the prevailing public attitude.

The first mistake came In August 1977, 10 months after Lerro became a member of the Tampa Bay Pilots' Association. It was a minor incident, no more significant than the metallic kiss of two bumpers in a crowded parking lot. No negligence by the pilot, the State Marine Casualty Review Panel reported.

Then 17 days later, on August 22, Lerro is piloting the Grace Boeing when a fierce thunderstorm whips up. It catches the vessel's lightened bow and pushes it aground. Lerro works the Grace Boeing free. There is no damage. Nevertheless, the rules require a formal report. The review panel finds no pilot error and takes no action.

On December 9 Lerro grounds the Stolt Advance. The Tampa division of the Coast Guard begins civil proceedings, but the district office in Miami dismisses the charges and closes the case without penalty. The grounding was abetted by three inoperable navigational aids, it is revealed.

1978 Is a good year for Lerro. No groundings, no collisions, no mistakes. The good fortune continued until April 1979. The Laurie U. and another one of those parking lot fender benders. Lerro brought the ship into an unfendered dock. There were six tires, too low, too far apart to prevent damage. No action by the review panel.

The good luck streak Lerro enjoyed for those 15 months seemed to disappear. He became like a baseball player in a slump. Every time he stepped up to do his job a bit of misfortune seemed to hang in the air.

- July 30, 1979: grounding, the Jersey Sun, fresh from extensive repairs. The steering mechanism goes awry soon after leaving the shipyard. The ship's master vouches for the vessel's poor performance. No action.
- December 3, 1979: collision, the Straits of Canso. A gantry crane and the railing of the ship touch while unmooring. The tugs and wind combine to help cause the error. The ship's master says so. No action against the pilot.
- February 16, 1980: Lerro Is attempting to pilot the largest Coast Guard-approved vessel permitted to sail the temporary channel. The 720-foot Jonna Dan swings to port to circumvent the salvage of the Blackthorn and fails to return starboard quickly enough. Lerro foresees the problem and drops anchor. The ship stops before the hole in the bridge. Wind and current push the stern into the bridge, chipping out a hunk of cement. Damages are estimated at $40,000. The review panel submits its findings to the 10-member State Board of Pilot Commissioners, five of whom are professional pilots. The commissioners report "action by pilot avoided collision; no action."

§ § § §

On Monday, while the rescue mission continues, Betty McCoy is back at it, bridge running once again. She drives from St. Petersburg to Bradenton in the morning and returns after school that afternoon. You only go 'round once in life, what the hell. Besides, the ride around the east side of the bay means an extra four hours travel time. Life must go on.

But not for Jim Pryor, the St. Petersburg resident who was delayed Friday morning because he forgot to put out the trash. The steam-powered crane hauled up the El Camino and dumped it unceremoniously on the barge. Then they pulled Pryor's body from the carnage.

63

Two more cars are hoisted from the depths and each contains a body. The body count goes up...26...27...28.

It increases every hour as reports come in from the massive search team assembled to walk 22 miles of shoreline and cruise 66 square miles of bay. A man's body is discovered floating near buoy 15, more than two miles from the bridge. Two women wash ashore on Mullet Key. Their corpses are found on the sand not 1,000 yards from one another. It is a stomach- wrenching scene as the corpses are hauled into Fort DeSoto Park after three days in the bay.

Late Monday afternoon Major Henderson of the sheriff's department makes it official: "That's it. We're going to secure. We figure we've got one, maybe two still missing and we feel they will float up. That will put the final total at 32 or 33."

What about the bus? The mystery has been solved. There was a bus of migrant farm workers, and they crossed the bridge Friday morning. They crossed all of the way to the other side and then the bus broke down, authorities explain.

Chapter 6
One of the Worst Ever

It seems official now: The Sunshine Skyway bridge disaster is not the worst in history. To put it in perspective the Associated Press reviews the nation's worst bridge disaster.

"Friday's accident at the Sunshine Skyway Bridge in Tampa Bay, Fla., is one of the worst bridge accidents in U.S. history," the Associated Press reports, and lists other bridge tragedies:

- Dec. 15, 1967: The Silver Bridge, 1,756-foot span over the Ohio River between Kanagua, Ohio, and Pt. Pleasant, W. Va., collapsed and sent trucks and autos plunging to the ground and into the river, killing 46 persons.
- June 16, 1964: The world's longest bridge, a causeway over Lake Pontchartrain north of New Orleans, was severed when two barges rammed into it. A 224-foot gap was torn in the 24-mile span and six persons aboard a Continental Trailways bus were killed when the bus fell into the river.
- Nov. 7, 1940: The Tacoma Narrows bridge, a suspension bridge buckled and crashed 190 feet into Puget Sound. The bridge, which became known as "Galloping Gertie," came apart in a 42- mile-per-hour wind. It occurred four months after the bridge was opened. No one was killed.
- Dec. 29, 1876: A bridge collapsed under a train in Ashtabula, Ohio, killing 92 persons.

Our obsession with statistics and ranking is satisfied. The Sunshine Skyway tragedy is given its rightful niche ("one of the worst bridge accidents in history") and is laid to rest in the record books, to be unburied only for new entries.

And here they come, numbers 32, 33, and 34, more bodies found Tuesday floating near Pinellas Point five miles northeast of the killer bridge.

Corpse 34 is identified as Tawanna McClendon, the young Tallahassee student who suffered from sickle cell anemia. Her strength and courage

65

serve no purpose any longer, for her personal fight has been ended in the early rounds by the killer bridge.

How many more bodies can there be out there in the bay? How many more water- logged, bloated corpses must we drag to shore? the rescue teams and public seem to be asking.

The answer comes quickly. The Coast Guard finds number 35 Wednesday.

"When the accident occurred, there was an outgoing tide, so chances are the bodies could be anywhere," a spokesman explains. Apparently, none remain in the tangled mass of steel and concrete beneath the bridge. All of the cars have been removed, including MacIntire's little pickup, the last of nine to be recovered.

The authorities are ready to concentrate now on clearing the channel. Commercial shipping interests are taking a beating. There is talk about laying off port workers unless something is done quickly. The barge-borne derrick can only handle 40 to 60-ton sections – mere chunks of the sections of steel girders that block the shipping lanes. The debris must be broken into smaller sections. The salvage experts must use explosives. Blow it up, haul it off, sell it as scrap, authorities decide.

For the rest of the week explosive charges are being detonated, 10 to 12 at a time, and the bay is boiling from the blasts. Traffic is stopped on the remaining span with each series of charges. When it does move, it moves slowly and in lesser numbers than when the bridge was whole. The amount of traffic crossing the Skyway dips to 10,000 vehicles per day, 20 percent less than before the accident.

A toll-taker speculates why motorists are staying away from the Skyway: "I think they are just chicken."

Chapter 7
The Blame Game

Thirty-five people died on May 9, 1980 because of:

A) Human error.
B) God
C) Bungling bureaucracy
D) All of the above

(Pick one of the above.)

A) Human Error

A special panel of the State Board of Pilot Commissioners did. They chose A, and said it was Pilot John Lerro's error that caused the Sunshine Skyway Bridge to tumble into Tampa Bay. The special panel of Pilot Commissioners supported the argument of a lawyer for the Florida Department of Professional Regulation.

The lawyer said Lerro "gambled" he could put the *Summit Venture* safely through the hole in the bridge. Like the careless horse player who squanders his fortune on a nag of a longshot, Lerro should have known better than to gamble the weather would clear by the time he reached the bridge, the lawyer implied.

The prudent pilot would have dropped anchor when visibility became limited. A careful mariner would have put the ship in full reverse and backed away from impending disaster. Lerro did none of these and that "amounts to incompetence and neglect," the lawyer argued.

"Captain Lerro took no action to halt the ship, change the course of the ship or drop anchors until the ship was in immediate peril of striking the bridge," he said.

"Captain Lerro had no idea where he was, no idea of how to get through the bridge and made no effort to stop. He took unnecessary risks and the bridge was struck," he said.

"It is our belief that in the approximate five minutes that passed (after the storm intensified), bringing the vessel to a halt was possible and could have easily been accomplished," he said.

The board heard Lerro's side of the argument and then without deliberation stated there was "probable cause" for revoking Lerro's license to pilot ships in Tampa Bay. It claimed John Lerro's negligence and incompetence caused the accident.

B) God did it

Not true, argued Lerro's lawyer. God did it. His invisible hand pushed the ship away from the hole in the bridge and caused it to ram the support pier. To prove it, Lerro' s lawyer called an expert, Bill Kowal, weatherman for WTVT-Channel 13, in Tampa, who used radar photographs, diagrams and charts to explain what occurred in the heavens the morning of May 9.

Heavy rain and strong winds descended upon Tampa Bay that morning. The rain may have been whipped by gusts up to 50 miles-per-hour and the wind direction may have shifted dramatically before the accident. That would explain why the *Summit Venture* strayed 800-feet from the middle of the channel.

From five to seven minutes before the tragedy, the wind on Anna Maria Island, six miles south of Egmont Key, gusted from the south and southwest at 48 to 50 miles-per-hour according to Kowal' s volunteer weather observers.

The winds on Pinellas Point east of the Skyway gusted up to 43 miles-per-hour between 7:15 and 7:30, four minutes before the *Summit Venture* felled the bridge.

The Lord works in strange ways, and on Friday, May 9, 1980, He had a hand in causing a catastrophe, was the logic applied by Lerro's attorney, Steven Yerrid.

To further prove mysterious events took place in the middle of the bay, Lerro's lawyer called for the testimony of a naval architect and of a mathematical wizard.

Both men came to the same conclusion: Some force acted upon the *Summit Venture* and moved it away from the channel.

The force pushed against the exposed hull of the ship. The *Summit Venture* dumped so much ballast while at anchor that more of its hull was above the water than below. Its bow rode 12 feet higher than its stern. The force, the wind, the hand of God, if you will, pushed the ship sideways at 3.8 feet per second which equals 800 feet in four minutes.

The hand of God had to move the ship off course because the ship's recorder - a roll of grid paper covered with flowing pen lines - shows the vessel was steered in a line that would put it in the channel and through the hole in the bridge, the experts testified.

Lerro's lawyer argued the accident was an act of God and no one – not the pilot, not the crew – can be held responsible for God's actions.

The owners of the *Summit Venture* also argued the accident was an act of God. They did so in a suit filed on May 19. Violent thunderstorms swept the bay without warning, making it impossible for mere mortals to overcome the force or the consequences thereof.

Absolve us from blame, the Liberian-based owners prayed to the court. It was the hand of God that caused this tragedy. Then as an afterthought, an admission maybe that God only used a finger or two, the owners asked that if found liable, damages be limited to $14 million, the value of the *Summit Venture*.

C) Bungling Bureaucracy.

How did bureaucracy cause the Sunshine Skyway catastrophe? Simply by its definition: government officialism and inflexible routine that ignores real needs.

The Florida Department of Transportation and the State Board of Pilot Commissioners overlooked a real need by failing to heed obvious warnings that a tragedy was in the making.

As early as 1971 the bureaucracy was warned about the questionable qualifications of pilots who worked Tampa Bay. State Rep. Tom Gallen, D-Bradenton, wrote Gov. Reubin Askew a letter pointing out an unqualified pilot "could cause irreparable damage to public and private property as well as endanger life."

Gallen, a lawyer, who later became a leading member of the state Senate until his 1978 resignation, urged the governor to investigate the licensing practices of what was then known as the Tampa Board of Pilot Commissioners. Gallen had received information that the board functioned like a fraternity and only those with connections to the brotherhood could become pilots.

No immediate action came from his call for an investigation, but it helped open up what had been a closed shop. The pilots' association ceased its buddy-buddy system and began hiring professionals who had no connections with the brotherhood.

John Lerro was one of the professional outsiders brought into the fraternity of pilots. The brotherhood protested Lerro's selection by the State Board of Pilot Commissioners. Some pilots were angry that Lerro was chosen over a local seaman who logged more than 7,000 trips in Tampa Bay. The protest failed, but the pilots' association registered its objection that other applicants were more qualified than Lerro.

Those warnings are mild compared to the statements issued six months prior to the Skyway tragedy. Capt. A. E. Schaefer, a member of the State Board of Pilot Commissioners, warned his colleagues in November 1979: "There appears to be a high incidence of casualties attributed to a small number of pilots. I suggest that we investigate some of these casualties and revoke the license of any incompetent pilot before a major catastrophe results."

Schaefer, a pilot and a retired Navy officer, was alarmed that Tampa Bay pilots had more accidents, or casualties, than all other state licensed pilots. He was concerned that the Board of Pilot Commissioners was too lenient. He launched his protest after the board dropped its investigation of a Tampa Bay pilot involved in 17 maritime mishaps in five years. "Incompetent pilots" are a hazard, Schaefer warned.

Since Its creation in 1975 the board registered 236 reports of maritime accidents by licensed pilots. One hundred and fifty-nine of those mishaps occurred when pilots from Tampa Bay were in command, making Florida's busiest shipping channel the most accident prone.

Never did the Board of Pilot Commissioners discipline a pilot, even though the Coast Guard handed out fines for negligence to pilots involved in some of those same incidents.

The Florida Department of Transportation also had plenty of warning about the consequences of May 9.

The warning the transportation bureaucrats received was much more real, much more frightening than any memorandum or letter of protest.

On May 2, 1978, the 75,000-ton Phosphate Conveyor, the largest vessel to regularly use the shipping channel, moved west toward the Sunshine Skyway. The pilot, John Schiffmacher, the same pilot who chose to anchor the *Pure Oil* in the face of the May 9 storm, had the giant vessel lined-up to sail beneath the Skyway. Then the vessel lost all power and Schiffmacher was helpless in efforts to steer the ship. Through skilled piloting and with the drag from the anchors, Schiffmacher was able to stop the Phosphate Conveyor from ramming the bridge broadside. Tragedy was avoided by 40 feet.

The near collision raised speculation about what might have happened if the ship had failed to stop in time. An investigation revealed many of the Skyway's support pilings were cracked and weak. A broadside blow from a ship the size of the Phosphate Conveyor might wipe out the entire bridge, sending the roadway spilling into the bay. There could be a great loss of life.

Why wasn't the bridge protected by an adequate fender system; barricades strong enough to stop a ship or slow it sufficiently to prevent a critical blow? A fender system was installed when the twin bridges were built originally but it deteriorated and crumbled away. Department of Transportation officials determined the replacement cost too exorbitant to justify a new fender system; instead, they decided to erect clusters of poles bound by steel cables.

The department's chief of maintenance best summed up the bureaucracy's attitude: "How far should we go in being our brother's keeper? Should we put armor plating over houses to protect them from airplanes? Shouldn't the ships themselves have some sort of backup system? They go through a lot of bridges?"

Twenty months later came the Blackthorn disaster, another indication something was wrong.

Then, finally, the near miss of the Jonna Dan with John Lerro In the pilot's seat.

There was plenty of warning that a disastrous catastrophe lurked in the future. All of the ingredients were there. They exploded like a time bomb on May 9 because no one – not John Lerro, not the Board of Pilot Commissioners, the Department of Professional Regulation, the Department of Transportation or the U.S. Coast Guard could know the future.

There also was a lack of diligence on the part of Michael J. Curtin, the driver of the ill- fated Greyhound bus, claims a $6 million lawsuit filed on behalf of Rosalee Randall, the mother of Tawanna McClendon, the college student on the bus the morning of May 9.

Bradenton attorney E. Clinch Kavanaugh III and his co-counsel, Robert Z. Trohn, captured headlines when they filed the first of numerous lawsuits resulting from the May 9 tragedy. Kavanaugh and Trohn named the Greyhound Bus Lines and Curtin as defendants. They argued Curtin "recklessly drove the bus at an excessive rate of speed, passing other vehicles that had stopped and slowed because of a blinding rainstorm in which there was no visibility, passing persons attempting to signal the bus to stop."

The lawyers also named the Department of Transportation, claiming it was negligent in its failure to provide a fender system to protect the bridge and motorists from off-course ships like the *Summit Venture*.

So, who Is to blame?

According to a survey by Premark Research Corp. of St. Petersburg, 28 percent of the 793 Tampa Bay residents questioned said John Lerro was at fault. Fifteen percent blamed the builders or engineers who designed and constructed a bridge that collapsed like a child's erector set. Thirteen percent said bad weather caused the accident. Nine percent said the tragedy was an act of God.

Include the bureaucracy and the answer becomes obvious:

D – All of the above.

Who do you blame?

Cast your vote and tell me why. You can reach me at SkywayJim1980@gmail.com. I'll publish your comment in the eBook version of SKYWAY.

Chapter 8
Something's Wrong

~~~

It will take at least until 1983 to reconstruct the Skyway just as It was. It may take the rest of the decade to do it right. Meanwhile, 25,000 people cross the Sunshine Skyway every day. In the back of their minds they must ask themselves: Could It happen to me?

~~~

"This committee should start at ground zero, with a clean blank slate," said State Rep. Elvin Martinez, the Tampa Democrat selected chairman of a special legislative committee assigned to investigate the Skyway tragedy.

"It would appear that we should first study three areas," asserted Martinez days after the disaster." One, is there something wrong with the shape and design of the channel itself? No. 2, is there something wrong with the design and shape of the bridge? No. 3, is there something wrong with the design and makeup of the pilots?"

Yes, something is wrong with the shape and design of the channel. At its most crucial point, a mere seven-tenths of a nautical mile west of the main span, the channel doglegs to the left. Massive ocean-going vessels must maneuver to make this 19-degree turn to port and they must do it quickly and accurately or else the Sunshine Skyway will be on top of them. When John Lerro received the sighting of turn buoy 2A, the *Summit Venture* was only seven boat lengths from the bridge. The margin for error was too slight. Records show there are fewer mishaps with vessels approaching from the east; the pilots have more than two miles to line-up with the hole in the bridge.

Doglegs are for golf courses, not shipping lanes that pass under heavily traveled bridges. The authorities can avoid future disasters by redesigning the channel and giving inbound vessels a chance to prepare properly to pass beneath the Skyway.

Yes, something is wrong with the design and shape of the bridge. The distance between the two main support piers - 800 feet - is too narrow. Again, there is not enough margin for error. A quarter of a century ago the hole in the bridge was adequate for vessels half the size of today's behemoths. The powers that be need only to look at other bridges: New York's Verrazano Narrows, San Francisco's Golden Gate, Maryland's Chesapeake Bay Bridge —all are two to five times wider than the hole in the Sunshine Skyway.

And the hole in the Skyway will grow smaller as the ships entering Tampa Bay grow bigger. More is needed, however.

The support piers need a fender system, or dolphins — rubber-encased pilings capable of deflecting or stopping a stray ship. Islands of soft sand need to be dredged from the bottom and piled around the base of the support piers. The sand sucked up from the dredging of a new channel can be used; then no more will Skyway motorists wonder if the next passing vessel is the one that will dump them into the bay.

Yes, something is wrong with the design and makeup of the pilots. They are protected by the bureaucrats. The state of Florida needs to appoint people who are willing to take action against pilots whose incompetence proves them a menace to the public safety. Most of the members of the Tampa Bay Pilots' Association are skilled seamen and the recent tragedies mar their reputations unfairly.

If the state of Florida corrects the hazardous conditions of the channel, redesigns and protects the Skyway, and regulates pilots adequately there will be no more catastrophes like the one that took 35 lives on May 9, 1980.

There is little doubt the state intends to accomplish this. But when? It will take at least until 1983 to reconstruct the Skyway just as it was. It may take the rest of this decade to do it right.

Meanwhile, 25,000 people cross the Sunshine Skyway every day. In the back of their minds they must ask themselves: Could it happen to me?

Chapter 9
Could it happen to me?

~~~

The MacFarland is in the shadows of the Sunshine Skyway...helpless... drifting uncontrollably towards the bridge...guided only by the hand of God. The captain sends men to the bow and orders them to standby the anchor. The port anchor plunges into the bay. Achingly-tense seconds tick by. Will the hooks grab the bottom...or will...?

~~~

Friday morning, June 13, 1980, the McFarland is westbound in the Tampa Bay shipping channel. Ahead are the wounded remains of the Sunshine Skyway Bridge, some of which clogs the normal channel and constricts it to the point where tugboats must assist vessels safely beneath the single remaining span.

Overhead, two-way traffic moves steadily in the morning rush hour. The bridge runners are out in force this time of day and it is as though a brightly colored metallic snake is crawling over the center span. It has been 35 days since the *Summit Venture* ripped away the southbound span, but motorists still slow to gawk at the destruction. In fact, the Sunshine Skyway is becoming a tourist attraction. People drive over aimlessly so they can tell the folks back home they saw the killer bridge. There is even talk of selling chunks of the felled superstructure as souvenirs.

No tugs accompany the McFarland. It is a special vessel, a dredge, and its sophisticated steering and propulsion mechanisms give the ship exceptional maneuverability. It is longer than a football field, weighs 6,000 tons, and moves like a waterbug.

A detail of traffic controllers is on the scene. They work in shifts and never leave their posts. They have been on duty since that tragic Friday morning In May. Using a mobile radio unit, they tell approaching captains when it is safe to sneak through the pinched hole in the bridge.

The time Is 7:55 a.m., and the McFarland has the green light to shoot the gap in the bridge. The sky is clear; visibility is 12 miles. The wind blows from the northeast at a steady 15 knots, pushing up half-foot seas.

77

One thousand yards west of the Skyway the steel hull of the McFarland slows its slide through the green-gray bay. Without warning, the energy that keeps the vessel alive in the water snaps off like an electric light.

The ship's automatic alarm system activates and the 73-man crew snaps to attention. A voice breaks through on the VHF marine channel. "We lost power..." the voice yells. The McFarland, with all of its fancy steering gizmos, is dead in the water. The captain is powerless to steer the vessel or even reverse its engines.

The McFarland is in the shadows of the Sunshine Skyway...helpless...drifting uncontrollably towards the bridge...guided only by the hand of God.

The captain sends men to the bow and orders them to stand by the anchor. The port anchor plunges into the bay. Achingly tense seconds tick by. Will the hooks grab the bottom...or will...?

The anchor buries into the bottom, the chain pulls taut and the McFarland stops 100 yards from the pilings of the bridge.

"That was close!" exclaims the voice on the radio.

Fifteen stories above the bay the tires of unsuspecting motorists hum on the metal grating of the Sunshine Skyway.

Chapter 10
Aftermath

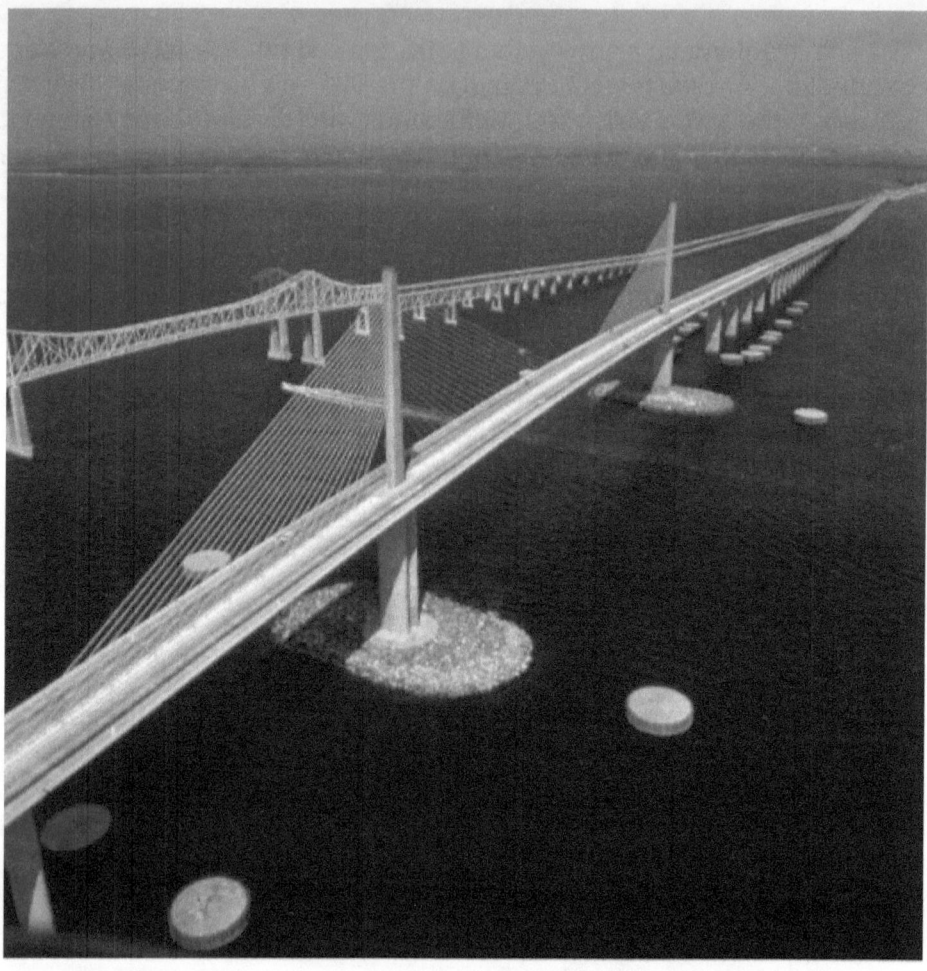

The vibe among Tampa Bay residents was strange in the days and weeks following the collapse of the region's most famous landmark.

What's going on? Never seen anything like it in all my years. Damn bridge must be cursed. Things are spinning out of control.

Shocked and unsettled described the mindset of locals in the first half of 1980. Who could blame them? Fifty-eight dead pulled from the bay in 100 days, all within the shadow of bridge. It was as though a strange force was drawing big ships to the Skyway and causing them to lose control.

All of a sudden the bridge was struck by three ships in four months, and two of those vessels were piloted by the same person. No wonder four out of 10 locals said they preferred to drive around the bay than over it.

On the night of January 28, the U.S. Coast Guard cutter Blackthorn collided with the Capricorn minutes after the oil tanker passed under the west span. Twenty-three of the 50 sailors on the Blackthorn perished when it sunk to the bottom of the channel.

Then 19 days later, Lerro bumped a support pier while navigating around the Blackthorn as it rested on the bottom of the channel. Eighty-one days later, he took out a quarter mile of concrete and steel. Thirty-six people took the plunge.

Other than occasional leapers heaving themselves over the rail and falling 150-feet into the bay, the Skyway made few headlines and provided little chatter. Post May 9, however, stories were hyped and circulated verbally about supernatural incidents – like the oft-repeated story about the guy who picked up a hitchhiker at the Pinellas County toll booth. After an uneventful trip across the lone span and conversation about the strange events of recent days, the hitchhiker disappeared once safe passage on the southern shore was gained. Other ghost stories made the rounds, and while the details varied, the theme remained the same: ghosts of the dead who were denied passage over the Skyway are rising from the bottom and hitching rides to complete their journey.

Meanwhile, local, state and federal officials focused on more down to earth matters.
On Sunday, May 11, the east span was opened to two-way traffic. For many, it took courage to make the journey. The real threat was not from an errant ship, but from rubber-necking drivers who looked at everything but the road ahead and oncoming traffic.

On May 12, a temporary channel – half as wide, half as deep as the original – was established so the busiest port in Florida could take care of business.

A state of emergency was declared by the governor for the three counties around the bay and its nearly 2 million residents.

Search teams worked to find bodies, with the final corpse retrieved May 14 near Anna Maria Island, miles from the bridge.

Newspaper circulation departments worked overtime to mail copies to snowbirds who couldn't get enough information up north.

In late May, the secretary of the Florida Department of Transportation declared the damaged span should be rebuilt. A series of concrete fenders should be added around the main piers for protection. It will take $37 million and 18-20 months to complete, he said. The announcement was met with strong push-back by local leaders and by their constituents who must use the bridge.

"Without consulting anyone in Pinellas or Manatee counties, without consulting anyone in the legislature, without consulting those responsible for the safe passage of ships and without consulting effectively with Congress, the bureaucrats have decided how they are going to rebuild the Skyway," the St. Petersburg Times editorialized. "They've chosen the quickest and cheapest alternative. That may be a mistake."

Feeling the pressure, the Florida legislature voted to delay the transportation department's decision for six months. Task forces were formed by leaders in the surrounding counties. The decision to build the missing quarter mile of bridge was put to rest once internal DOT documents revealed cracks in bridge's pilings.

The task forces looked at the possibility of digging a tunnel beneath Tampa Bay.

That option died quickly when it was revealed the project would take 10 years, cost half a billion dollars, and jack the toll to $15.

A proposal to deep-six both exiting spans and build a new 4-to-8 lane structure gained popularity when it was discovered the federal government would open its checkbook if the approaching roadways and the new bridge were built to interstate standards.

On Jan. 31, 1981, it was announced a cable-stayed, modernistic structure built to interstate standards and with safety-related improvements was the way to go. It would cost $215 million, rise 194 feet above the channel to accommodate bigger ships, and the channel width would increase 50% to 1,200 feet. Round concrete pilings 60 feet in diameter would be planted 20 feet into the bay bottom. Stone islands to deflect wayward ships would stand watch over the main support piers. Phase 1 was scheduled to begin in 1982.

While the engineers were hard at work, so were the lawyers.

The families of 14 victims sued Greyhound, claiming driver Michael Curtin caused the demise of their loved ones through recklessness. A jury disagreed.

Greyhound then sued the owner of the *Summit Venture*, Hercules Carriers, for $200 million. Hercules sued Greyhound and the State of Florida. The State of Florida sued Hercules for $23 million and in 1984 was awarded $19 million.

The lawyers representing the kin of the deceased lined up for damage awards. $1.5 million went to the relatives of a Tampa businessman. $1.2 million was awarded to the 20-year-old paraplegic son who lost his parents and primary caregivers on May 9. Most damage awards were in the $300,000 range. Wesley MacIntire, the sole survivor, was paid $175,000.

Meanwhile, on the east side of the bay near Apollo Beach, a scrap dealer purchased the concrete and steel remains of the bridge. A piece of broken steel girder or a chunk of concrete – the perfect souvenir or a good paperweight – went for as little as $1.

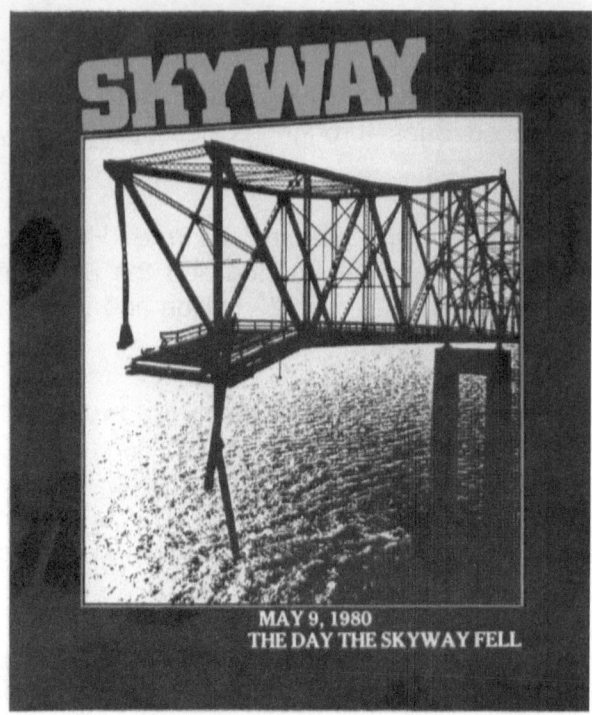

MAY 9, 1980
THE DAY THE SKYWAY FELL

A reporter for the Sarasota Herald-Tribune, Jim Curtis, one of the first persons to reach the summit of the northbound span after the accident, published SKYWAY in December 1980. The magazine-format publication featured 32 on-scene photographs and an in-depth account of the accident. It was distributed on newsstands and in grocery stores throughout the Tampa Bay region and quickly sold 30,000 copies.

"As bureau chief of the Herald-Tribune's Bradenton office, I followed the aftermath for weeks and months. It was a story that would not go away. Plus, the circulation department was flooding the newsroom with calls from out-of-state people who wanted more information, so I knew there was tremendous interest.

"In what was really wishful thinking, I put a banner on the front cover of SKYWAY that said, 'Collector's Edition $3.50'. Little did I know," Curtis said. "Last I heard, recycled original copies from 40 years ago sell online for $25-$100."

The new, improved Sunshine Skyway Bridge opened to traffic in April 1987. The original bridges were demolished four years later. The causeways that led to the twin spans were converted into fishing piers.

"When people think of Florida in the future, it may well be Disney, the Cape (Canaveral), and the Skyway," declared designer Eugene Figg.

The new sleek Skyway stood as a symbol that Tampa Bay had arrived as a major metropolitan area and had achieved that status in record time. Thirty-four years earlier, the only way across the bay was by ferry.

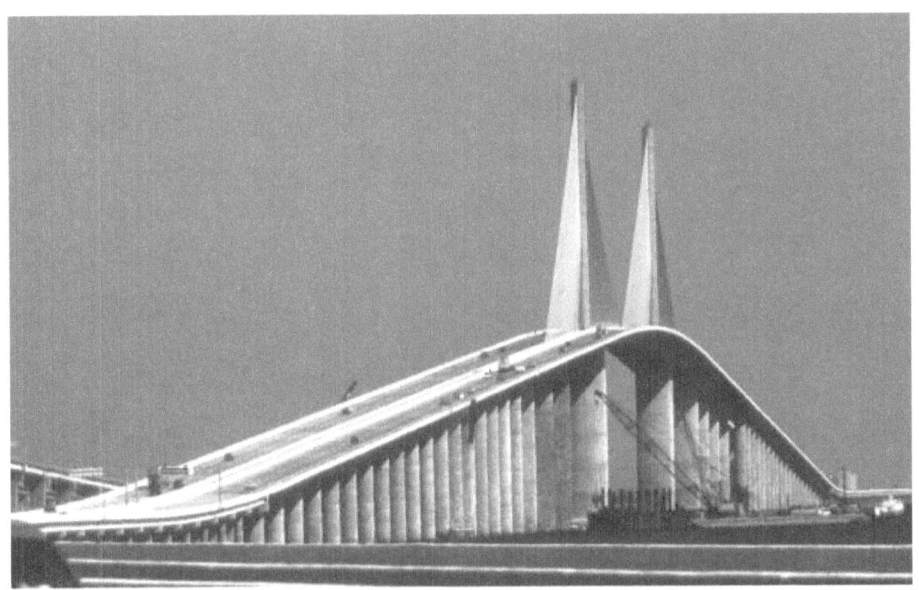

Four decades later, the incredible story of the demise of the Skyway still lived.

"The Skyway Bridge Disaster" documentary debuted in the fall of 2019. It took a closer look at what happened on May 9 and in the aftermath. The 110-minute documentary took viewers onto the bridge, inside the ship, and into the courtroom. The film highlighted experiences from survivors and local leaders, as well as Steven Yerrid, a co-producer and the lawyer who represented Lerro.

"He told me a couple of times he wished he was one of the people who died that day," Yerrid told a reporter for Fox 13 Tampa. "That's hard to hear from someone you loved. And I actually loved him. We became like brothers."

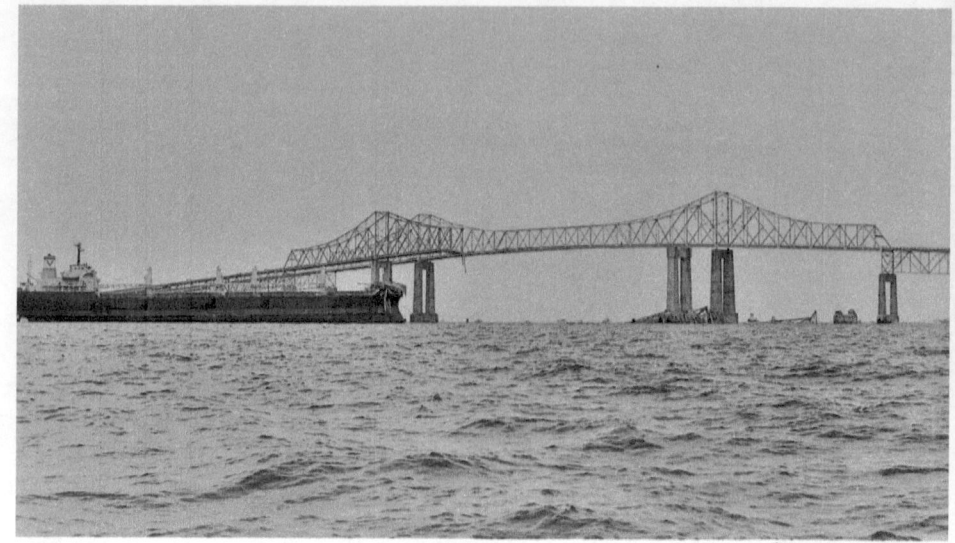

The Summit Venture

The *Summit Venture* sailed under the broken Sunshine Skyway Bridge on May 30, 1980 – accompanied by two tugs and without incident. Laden with 31,000 tons of crushed phosphate rock, it cruised past Egmont Key and headed for the South Pacific.

Despite the loss of 35 lives, hundreds of millions in damages, dozens of lawsuits, and its role in one of the worst ship-bridge accidents in world history, the *Summit Venture* was back in business. It sailed under the same name until 1993 when its Chinese owners renamed it.

In 2010, while carrying iron ore, it was hit by high winds and heavy seas off the coast of Vietnam. The crew of 27 abandoned ship. The 608-ft freighter rests on the bottom of the ocean.

Wesley MacIntire
Sole Survivor

Thirty-six unsuspecting souls were dumped into the water 150 ft below the Sunshine Skyway Bridge that day in May. Only one survived. It was the second time in his 56 years on the planet Wesley MacIntire cheated death. The Springfield, Massachusetts native enlisted in the Navy as a 17-year-old and on June 6, 1944 found himself in a landing craft storming the beaches of Normandy, France. A projectile from German artillery ripped through the vessel, sinking it, and dumping MacIntire and his combat-ready buddies into the surf. Under intense fire, MacIntire made his way to another landing craft and eventually made it to the beach. The sole survivor of his unit on D- Day, MacIntire escaped the fate of the 4,414 allied forces killed in 24 hours.

MacIntire survived the collapse of the Skyway when his Ford mini-pickup landed on the bow of the *Summit Venture*, bounced off, and sunk to the bottom of the bay. MacIntire relied on his Navy survival training to escape and swam 40 feet to the surface. With blood running from a gash in his forehead, he grabbed a fallen girder under the northbound span and yelled for help. A crewman from the *Summit Venture* tossed a lifeline and MacIntire was pulled out of the bay at 7:55 am, 20 minutes after his historic plunge.

Following a brief stay at St. Anthony's Hospital, MacIntire was up and about, trying to put the pieces of his life together.

He and his wife of 35 years, Betty, visited the *Summit Venture* at the Port of Tampa, where it was undergoing repairs. The couple presented the crew with a cake decorated with English and Chinese lettering that spelled "Thank You." MacIntire posed for a photograph with the crewman who pulled him from the bay.

He also posed for another photo – this time days later with his battered truck at a junkyard where vehicles lifted from the bottom of Tampa Bay were stored.

In July, MacIntire flew to New York City to become a contestant on the popular game show "To Tell The Truth." Two of the four judges found his incredible story true.

On the morning of May 9, 1981, MacIntire and his wife walked out on the damaged, closed bridge with a bundle of flowers. They waited for the southbound Greyhound and waved as it motored by on the remaining span. Thirty-five carnations, one for each victim, were dropped into the bay. It was an act of devotion repeated each May 9 for the remainder of MacIntire life.

In May 1984, MacIntire received $175,000 as settlement from the owners of the *Summit Venture*.

On Oct 14, 1989, MacIntire, 65, died of cancer. His ashes were spread over Tampa Bay.

John Lerro
Victim or Villain?

On June 17, 1980, one day before John Lerro's return to piloting big ships under the Skyway Bridge, the Florida Department of Professional Regulation suspended Lerro's license because the pilot "lacked the necessary skill, judgement, and presence of mind to pilot a vessel in a trustworthy manner."

The Department of Professional Regulation ruled Lerro failed to "properly react" on May 9 and "this demonstrates that John Lerro does not possess the ability to execute command of a vessel in a stressful situation and should he continue to pilot vessels on Tampa Bay, lives and property will be unnecessarily jeopardized."
Lerro's attorney, Steven Yerrid, appealed and lost. A full hearing was scheduled for October, where Lerro would be stripped of his license or fully exonerated.

A good portion of Tampa Bay residents breathed a collective sigh of relief. A poll showed that 28% of them believed Lerro was at fault. Furthermore, 42% said they intended to avoid driving over the bridge.

Lerro, his wife, and their teen son reportedly went into hiding for several weeks after the accident to avoid the glare of negative publicity. Nevertheless, the slander of the 37-year-old pilot continued to buzz: he was a drunk who liked ballet and classical music; an outsider from New York who was incompetent, who should have been terminated for his lousy record.

Indeed, reports showed Lerro was cited for seven incidents in four years while piloting on Tampa Bay. Five of the seven incidents were determined to be unavoidable, including the most severe, which occurred in February,1980 when Lerro nicked a piling of the bridge while piloting the 720-foot Jonna Dan, chipping off a hunk of concrete and doing $40,000 damage. A review by the Board of Pilot Commissioners reported "action by pilot avoided collision; no action."

Less attention was focused on the fact that Lerro's record was better than several other Tampa Bay pilots, who managed to rack up 17, 11, and 10 incident reports.

The Hillsborough County state attorney announced he was considering criminal charges. A review of the facts showed no crime was committed – despite the loss of life and the ruin of $200-$300 million in state property, the state attorney ruled.

The hearing in October at the Hillsborough County Courthouse in Tampa lasted four days. The prosecutor for the state claimed "the (*Summit Venture*) was not blown into the Skyway Bridge. It was steered into the bridge."

Yerrid countered by arguing the tragedy was caused by an act of God, which he defined as "a force of nature occurs that is unexpected, and so intense, and so supervening, as to relieve the human actions taken under the overpowering influence of that force." John Lerro could not be found negligent, Yerrid argued, "if there was a finding this bridge was brought down by an act of God."

On Christmas Eve, the hearing officer exonerated the defendant in full.

In April 1981, Lerro reported to duty for the first time in 11 months. He boarded a tug at the Port of Tampa that powered a 501-foot barrage filled with gasoline. Lerro piloted the vessel past the ghostly remains of the Skyway Bridge three hours later.

Returning to a normal life was impossible for the 38-year-old pilot. He was diagnosed with multiple sclerosis, an incurable, chronic auto-immune disease that attacks and damages the central nervous system. It wasn't long before the duties of a harbor pilot became overwhelming. Lerro applied for and received an extended leave of absence from the Tampa Bay Pilots' Association.

His wife moved out soon after and took their teen son with her. Lerro lost his occupation, his family, and his health before his 40th birthday.

In January 1985, Lerro joined the faculty of the State University of New York Maritime College, his alma mater. He taught basic seamanship and advanced ship handling for two semesters.

The next year he returned to the Tampa Bay area and showed up at a press conference arranged by Yerrid to announce the making of a movie, "An Act of God," the story of a young attorney and his client accused of causing one of the worst ship-bridge disasters in history.

"This is dealing with an angry man, about how miserable my 42 years on this planet turned," Lerro told the assembled media. "Sure, it may be a little soul-selling, making money on a mistake. But what about the victims' relatives? They sat through court hearings and took the money. They took it.

"I think the movie may piss people off. If it does, okay. If they come after me, it won't be the first time and I'll be ready.

"What I hope now is that the story will at least make me a human being. in some people's eyes, I stopped being that six years ago."
The movie was never made.

Lerro enrolled in the University of South Florida's College of Education and attended classes, using a cane to get around campus. He received a master's degree and worked for the Hillsborough County Counseling Center. They parted ways after a brief stint.
In 1987, Lerro divorced. The judge granted him $500 month in alimony.

As his debilitating disease took its toll, Lerro became less active and spent time reading and writing. He needed a housekeeper to assist him in activities of daily living. In 1998, he married her, a 39-year-old German woman named Laila.

By 2001, Lerro was wheelchair bound.

In August 2002, he went into a coma and died the last day of the month at age 59.

His wife Laila told the Tampa Tribune, "He spoke to me frequently about it and he never forgave himself. I hope he found forgiveness for himself in the end. He was an incredibly kind man."

"He was a client," said Yerrid, in a 2019 interview with Fox 13 Tampa. "He was me. And in the end, we were brothers," Yerrid said, with tears in his eyes.

Chapter 11
Where were you the day the Skyway fell?
Reporter's Notebook

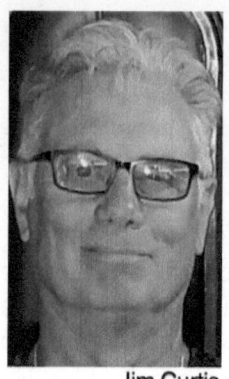
Jim Curtis

On Friday, May 9, 1980 at 7:34 a.m. – the official day, hour and minute the Sunshine Skyway Bridge plummeted into Tampa Bay – I was sleeping soundly in my home in Bradenton, Florida.

Sleeping soundly... until my wife woke me with the announcement, "Gene Page is on the phone and he says it's important."

"Tell him I'll call him back," I mumbled. "I think you better talk to him now."

Through the fuzz of semi-consciousness, I only got the gist of Gene's excited chatter..."something big at the Skyway...people in the water...I'm heading there in my boat..."

I hung up the phone and headed back to bed. I wasn't due in the newsroom for another two hours, and I was confident Gene, the most aggressive spot news photojournalist known to man, would run down what probably would be a wild goose chase or return to the darkroom later in the day with outstanding photos.

Five minutes later my wife reappeared. "It's Sherry." Instantly, I realized I was going to be part of something big. Sherry, one of our most soft spoken, mild-mannered reporters, never called me at home unless it was important. "You'd better get into the newsroom...I'm headed there now."

A cup of coffee, calls to the staff, and I was out the door. At the last moment, I threw my bike into the back of the family station wagon. Experience taught me the authorities always sealed off the scene. If I couldn't get to the bridge on four wheels, I might be able to reach it on two.

The news team of the Sarasota Herald-Tribune's Bradenton bureau was Skyway bound. The emergency vehicles were out in full force as we approached the toll booth of the northbound span. A Florida Highway

Patrol trooper waved us off the road and provided details.

"Not even emergency vehicles are permitted on the bridge at this time," he reported. "It's possible the northbound bridge was damaged and may be unsafe. The Skyway is closed to all vehicular traffic. Wait here and I'll let you know when you are authorized to access the accident scene," he said.

"Is it okay to ride my bike to the top of the bridge?"

It felt like a dumb question. I expected a less than cordial reply from the trooper. "Be my guest," he said.

The gloating lasted until I was alone on the bridge. The wind was sharp, a mist stung my face. Fog covered the bay. Visibility was 10 yards. Waves slapped the pilings in an eerie, rhythmic sound. All I could do was keep my head down and pump the pedals harder. Then my mind started playing games.

What if the trooper got bad information and a piece of the northbound bridge is missing? Surely, I could stop before I went over the edge? When is the sun going to shine? Where is the ship? Where are the dead bodies? Why am I here by myself? I've got a wonderful wife, two cute little kids and a mortgage. I felt like I was watching an episode of the supernatural TV thriller from the '60s and any minute Rod Serling would appear before me on the bridge; as the creepy music increased in volume he would announce, "Welcome....to The Twilight Zone." At least I would have company.

Suddenly, I heard a hum. It grew into a low roar. A motor? A Coast Guard cutter? A helicopter? Another errant ship? A motor vehicle? Yes, a loud one…behind me. I hopped off the bike and drew close to the guard rail. Out of the fog and mist came a Florida Department of Transportation truck, a big yellow one, headed to the top of the bridge and filled with people waving at me. Creepy Rod was nowhere in sight, just the reporters I left 15 minutes early. The truck stopped, I tossed my bike in the back, and rode the last mile to the top with the news team.

I believed my eyes, but the sight was incomprehensible: a Greyhound bus 150 feet below my feet, upside down, surrounded and supported by steel girders, its massive tires just below the surface; divers stood on its belly, then dove in search of bodies as oil bubbled up and put a sheen on the bay; the *Summit Venture*, its bow littered with girders and roadway, was anchored several hundred yards away, with two tugs pinned to its port side. The scene looked like jet fighters from MacDill Air Force Base just up the bay in Tampa mistakenly bombed a quarter mile of bridge.

The rain stopped; the sky cleared. We came, we saw, we left. It was mid-morning. The early deadline was only six hours away.

—Jim Curtis, Sun City Center, FL

(The following is an excerpt from David Klement's book "*The Life I Have Made*." Copyright 2019, David Klement)

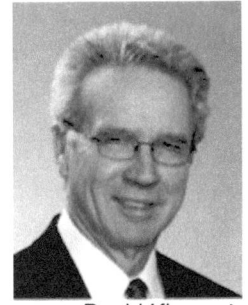

David Klement

The early morning of May 9, 1980, felt like a day without a dawn. Going outside to fetch something from the car at about 7:30 a.m., I was struck by the pitch darkness of the sky, as if the night hadn't ended at its normal time. That inky blackness, I would come to learn, would be the cause of – and fitting backdrop for – the horror that was to come.

It was so dark, my wife and I discussed the wisdom of letting the kids walk to the bus stop, all of 200 feet from our front door. As we scurried to get their lunches packed and backpacks organized, we volleyed over who was in the better position to drive them to school. She had an early appointment outside the office; I had my usual Friday morning crunch of preparing Opinion Page content for the weekend editions of the Bradenton Herald.

As I scanned the black sky for some sign of the oncoming storm's direction, little did I know that, within a few minutes, my routine would be turned upside down and I would be facing one of the most incredible news events of my career.

Journalists are famous for their gallows humor. Witness to so much tragedy, we often resort to wisecracks to ease the stress of a particularly gruesome news event. For as long as I had been working at the Herald, an editor or reporter leaving the building would say, "I'm going to the dentist. Call me if the Skyway falls." Or, "I'm going home for the day. Don't call me unless the Skyway falls."

There was no hysteria and very little emotion as we worked to cover the story of a lifetime. Professional instincts – and adrenaline – kicked in to overcome the shock of the event; the atmosphere in the newsroom was business-like. Later, though, pent-up emotions would give way to shock. One former copy editor admits today that, after finishing her shift, she went home and wept, thinking about the victims: "It was one of the few stories I ever cried over."

— David Klement, Bradenton, FL

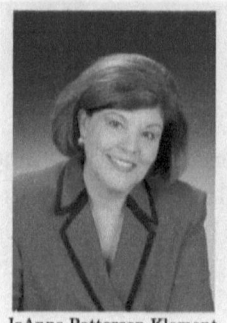

JoAnne Patterson Klement

To paraphrase the beloved Snoopy of the Peanuts gang: "It was a dark and stormy morning, the day the Skyway Bridge fell," I perfectly recall.

I was in the kitchen preparing breakfast for our two grade school kids; ages 10, and seven.

Viewing the almost black skies out the windows, my immediate thought was, "I don't think they should go out and stand at the school bus stop, which was exactly one house away. The mood of the weather was ominous in my mother's brain, always in the alert mode for kid safety. The sense that something was not right was palpable. It was spooky.

Because of the children's school schedule, I was the first to arrive at the Manatee Bureau of the Sarasota Herald-Tribune on Sixth Avenue in Bradenton. My desk was situated by the front door, and the police radio was in the far corner, strategically placed next to the police reporter's desk. Typically it was squawking some chatter, mostly unintelligible if you were not fluent in police jargon. I never really paid attention to it.

But this morning I heard "Skyway Bridge" loud and clear. It caught my ear and that minute our city editor, Jim Curtis, walked in and I alerted him to "something happening on the Skyway Bridge."

He listened for about 30 seconds, and we immediately agreed we needed to get there ASAP. We hopped into my pale green, 1973 Chevrolet station wagon with wood grain sides. Pre SUV days. Jim threw his bike in the back, and I drove.

We parked at the foot of the bridge as officials waved at us indicating "no cars."

Jim grabbed his bike, literally leaving me in his dust without a word of advice or instruction. "Darn him," I thought.

I had been a reporter exactly two years, with no prior experience at writing or reporting. Especially not covering accidents of this grand magnitude and seriousness.

My beat was the soft stuff: school board news, features, social events. But, instinct kicked in, and I followed him right up the bridge. In two-inch heels and what we called a "straight" skirt. Not an easy task.

When I reached the top, the road was like mesh, not a solid surface. I peered directly down and there was what appeared as one of my son's Match Box vehicles. The bottom, grey in color, was identical to one of his cars, I thought. But it was a Greyhound bus containing 22 passengers and a driver. I still recall that image.

Fortunately, I did not dwell on their tragic fate.

But, I think in the moment of serious news reporting, your brain kicks into a special gear that allows you to keep moving and focusing on the task at hand.

The more experienced reporters took over the writing of the main story, and I was assigned an accessory story covering other aspects of the tragedy. I liked my story assignment, which was talking to a young high school teacher about how he escaped by minutes driving over the bridge that fateful morning. In this day of grey and despair, here was a happy note.

Terry Butterfield routinely drove each morning to Manatee County from St. Petersburg for his teaching job. He was delayed from his usual timing by having to iron a pair of slacks after noticing a spot on the pair he was wearing.

"Thirty seconds earlier and that would have me down there," he said, referring to the people who drowned in Tampa Bay. "Now, I think of all the trivial things I did this morning. I ironed a second pair of pants. I took some vitamins, and that wasted some time. I shut off the water heater, and that wasted some time. I guess I'm one of the fortunate ones."

But, what really saved this young man's life was the driver in the car ahead of him who noticed the bridge was out. Because of the poor visibility, it was hard to realize there was no road ahead. There was no there there.

"I was disappointed in the weather," Butterfield recalled. "It was the worst I had ever seen on the Skyway. It was vicious, and it wasn't raining straight. It was pretty intense wind.

"When I got to the top of the bridge I noticed there was a man in a blue car stopped in the right hand lane. He was waving frantically.
"I figured he was out of gas and would need a ride to the gas station. I kept thinking, ' I am going to be late for work.'

"But, I remembered from church just this past week about the story of the Good Samaritan. I wasn't planning to stop, but I slowed down and stopped maybe 15 yards ahead of him. I backed in next to him and thought, 'Oh, geez I don't want to get out in the rain.'

"I got out, and he had his window rolled down, and I asked him, 'What is the problem?'

"He just simply said, 'The bridge has collapsed.'

"I kinda did a double take. I asked him, 'Are you serious?' It didn't hit me that that could happen; that that was a possibility.'

"He said, 'I just saw a bus and two cars go over, and I don't know how many more.' By this time my jaw was halfway to the ground."

"I picked myself back up and started running back down the bridge, flailing my arms as hard as I could.

"People would stop dead in their tracks."

"The good Lord was smiling on me, He was smiling hard on me," Butterfield concluded.

— JoAnne Klement, Bradenton, FL

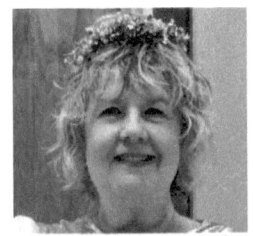

Janet Kerley

Just as first responders must steel themselves to do their jobs in the midst of pain, suffering and death, so must news reporters and photographers.

Four months earlier in January 1980, I had been sent to Ft. DeSoto near the mouth of Tampa Bay to write a story about recovery efforts of the Coast Guard Cutter Blackthorn, which had sunk after a collision in the shipping channel near the Skyway. Black body bags were being unloaded from small boats onto the wooden dock as I tried to interview officials about details.

Now on this rainy May morning I was driving to work at the Herald-Tribune bureau when I heard a radio announcer say there was a report that the Sunshine Skyway Bridge was down and there were cars in the water. I thought it had to be a joke—fake news.

We didn't have cell phones in those days, so I hurried to the bureau and called editor John Hamner at home to make sure he had heard and was assembling the troops. It was all hands-on deck as decisions were made about trying to charter boats or rent helicopters.

I was assigned to go to the Trailways Bus Station because there were reports that a bus had driven off the bridge. My job was to talk to relatives who might be waiting for the bus to arrive. It took an hour or so of confusion at the small bus station to figure out that it had actually been a Greyhound bus. I hurried across town to Greyhound, but didn't find anyone waiting on arrivals. Turns out that the one local passenger on the bus was 20-year-old Tawanna McClendon, a Tallahassee community college student on her way home to Palmetto to celebrate Mother's Day. I didn't see her family until the following week when I was assigned to attend her funeral service.

In the meantime, I was back on the dock in Ft. DeSoto interviewing divers and recovery workers as once again bodies in black bags were being unloaded from small boats after being freed from the tangled wreckage under the remaining bridge span. I remember asking myself how it was possible that I was once again standing on the edge of Tampa Bay watching such a gruesome scene unfold.

I felt very conspicuous intruding on the grief that permeated the church where the funeral was held for Tawanna McClendon. Weeping and wailing reverberated loudly as the preacher attempted to console her family and friends. At the cemetery afterwards, I recall her sobbing mother literally throwing herself across her daughter's coffin as it was perched above the open grave. It was heart- wrenching.

A couple of years later, I covered the civil trial in Tampa as families attempted to receive compensation from Greyhound. Testimony attempted to assign blame to bus driver Michael Curtin, who himself had perished. It was difficult to remain objective as I interviewed his distraught wife in the courthouse. The next day, I passed her a note of encouragement.

This tragedy was one of the biggest stories that local reporters ever had to cover. Our job was to observe the aftermath and share the personal stories with the public. But the emotional impact on us reporting the news is still there this many years later.

— Janet Kerley, Bradenton, FL

Where were you
the day the Skyway fell?

Most of us remember where we were and how we felt when major events occurred.

Beside May 9, 1980, two other dates are remembered always: November 22, 1963 and September 11, 2001.

I was in 10th grade geometry class when a young president was assassinated in Dallas. Thirty-eight years later, I was in Nova Scotia, Canada, waiting to catch a flight home when the twin towers fell on 9/11.

If you lived in the Tampa Bay region – or ever drove the Skyway Bridge – and were born before 1970, you probably remember where you were and how you felt when you heard the tragic news.

Let me and others know where you were and how you felt that day in May 1980. I'll publish your remarks in the digital version of SKYWAY. Send a selfie, too. I can be reached at SkywayJim1980@gmail.com.

From the author

I hope you enjoyed reading SKYWAY – if it is possible to enjoy reading about and seeing photographs of such a tragic event. Please take time from your busy schedule to write a review. It means a lot to me. The higher the overall rating and the more good reviews from readers like you, the more exposure SKYWAY receives.

In retrospect, there seems to be little good and a lot of bad associated with the Skyway Bridge disaster. Thirty-five people died horrible deaths. It is easy to feel the pain of those who loved them and, in a twinkling of an eye, lost them. Except for the grace of God, there go we.

The positive that came from such a terrible tragedy rises up out of Tampa Bay. The new Skyway Bridge is a shiny beacon for all to see. More importantly, it is a huge improvement over the structures that were built in 1954 and in 1971, respectively. Flat out, those bridges were unsafe. The new cable-stayed, four-lane Skyway built in 1987, with its islands and protective concrete columns, seems safer. The old Skyway was a tragedy waiting to happen.

Personally, crossing Tampa Bay has been an important part of my life. The first time was in the early '50s. A car ferry ran from near the current site of Port Manatee to St. Petersburg. It was leisurely, scenic and slow. Prior to 1971, motoring across the single span was a white- knuckle experience for me because of oncoming traffic and my apprehension that drivers looked at everything but the road ahead. My most horrifying experience came in the late '70s on the northbound span. As I crested the top at 60-mph, I avoided rear-ending a stopped car by blindly switching lanes. I stopped cursing when I realized the driver's door was wide open and the driver was in the bay.